Paint and Glow by Davina

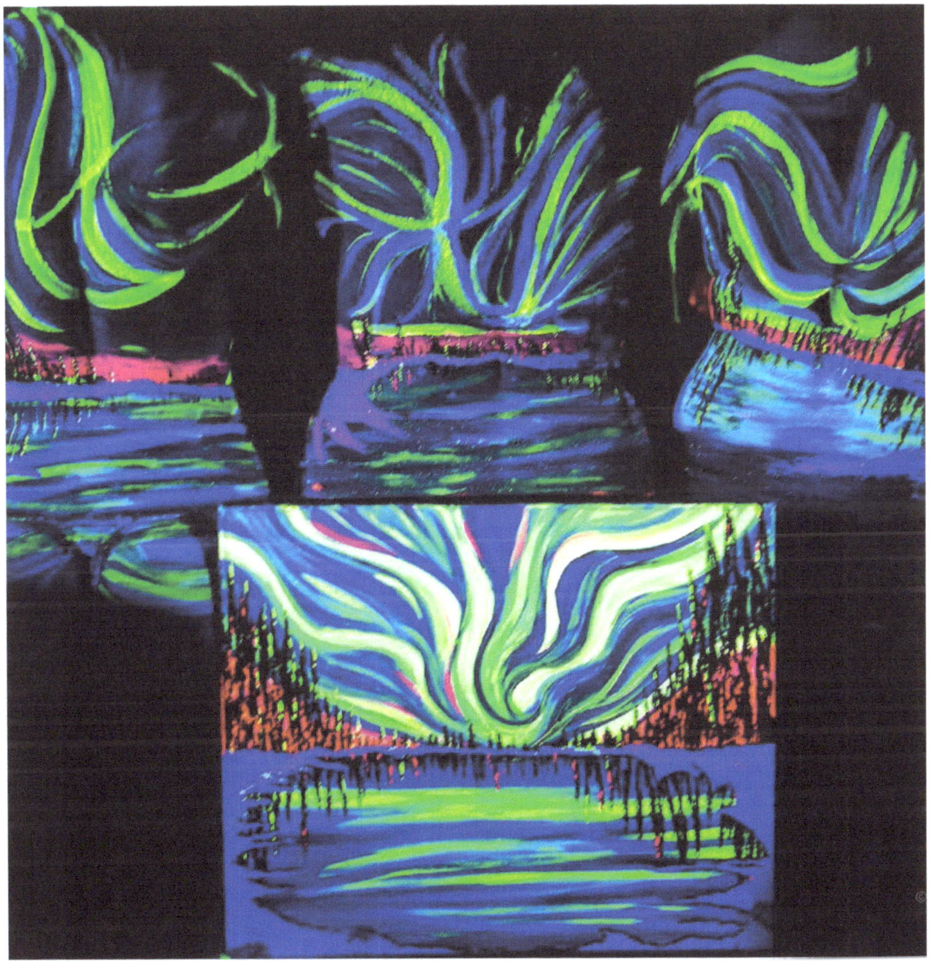

By Bradley Zink

DEDICATION

I would like to dedicate this book to all with an interest in art. Both young and old, all who explore the wonders of art, will have a deeper understanding of the beautiful world we live in.

Acknowledgements

I would like to thank my dear friend, Davina, for working with me to put together this incredible collection of her artwork.

Also, I would like to thank the incredible photography throughout this book to the gifted talents of:

Daniel Pham Photography

Julia Alicia Photography

Miriam Figueroa

Jose Islas Photography

Finally, I would like to thank the beautiful body art models Bette Bennett, Becca Smith, Alisha Marie, and Vincent Perez .

Without their contributions of 'art', this book would not have been possible!

About Paint and Glow
by Davina

Paint and Glow by Davina is a one of a kind painting experience. She has been painting since she was only 11 years old. While living In Manchester, England, she was taken under the wing of her high school teacher and taught an array of different artistic styles and techniques.

Utilizing her artistic imagination and education she's received through the years, she has continually been sharing her knowledge and experience with artistically driven and curious individuals. Davina helps people who not only want to learn how to paint, but do so in a unique and creative way, as well as learn the steps and techniques they need to create a masterpiece in their first class.

Davina is very passionate about her work and spreading the joy that comes from painting. During her classes, she works closely with every single person to ensure that their experience is both satisfying and joyful.

At Paint and Glow by Davina, you'll get to enjoy the most unique painting experience. With glow in the dark paint and UV blacklights, you can create a stunning masterpiece in just one class! All skill levels and ages are welcome for most classes.

Davina's group classes are perfect for friends and family that want to spend time together while cultivating their creative sides. Classes can be found at different venues, making them perfect for various groups that enjoy drinking and painting in San Diego. One of the most popular classes involves painting in bars, in which attendees get the opportunity to enjoy drinking and painting in fun and inspiring atmospheres.

Paint and Glow by Davina is a supporter of the San Diego community. Classes can be found all throughout the month in a variety of different venues across the city. By changing venues, those that attend her classes will get to experience different cultures and atmospheres throughout the city. She was a featured guest at The Best of San Diego Party in 2015.

Davina also enjoys contributing to the community through charity events, children's events, and by partnering with local hotels and restaurants. She knows through experience that art is therapeutic and has seen art therapy ease the minds of people in need.

One thing that she firmly believes is that art contributes to the cognitive thinking and social skills for children. She continues to volunteer her services with many of the charity foundations in and around San Diego.

Davina also offers children's painting classes catered towards imaginative children who are interested in learning how to paint. She has worked with special needs children and has volunteered at Rady's Children's Hospital. Parents with children of all ages are encouraged to enroll their children in paint and glow classes to show them a new side of painting they have never seen before.

http://paintandglowbydavina.com/

http://juliaaliciaphotography.com

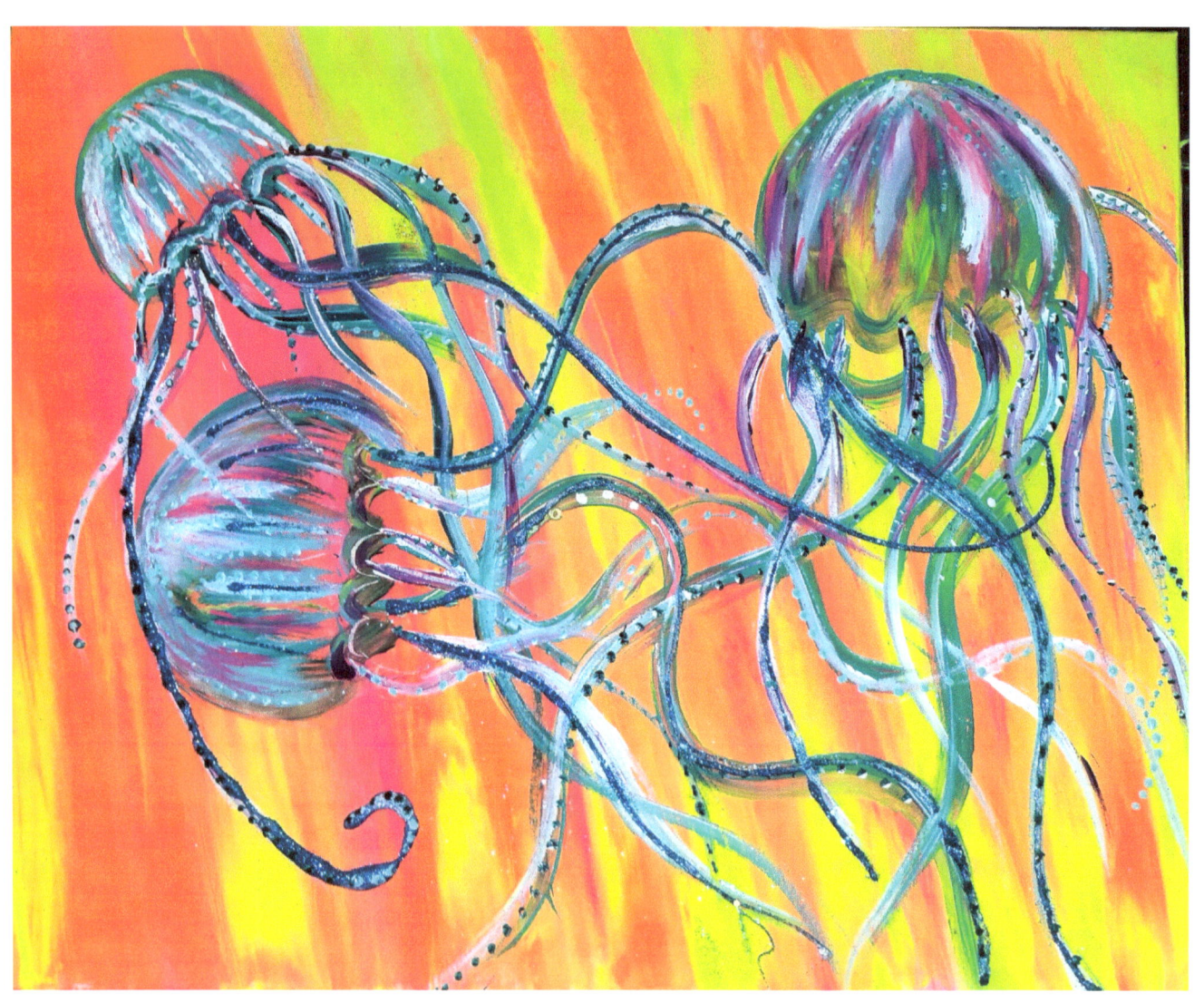

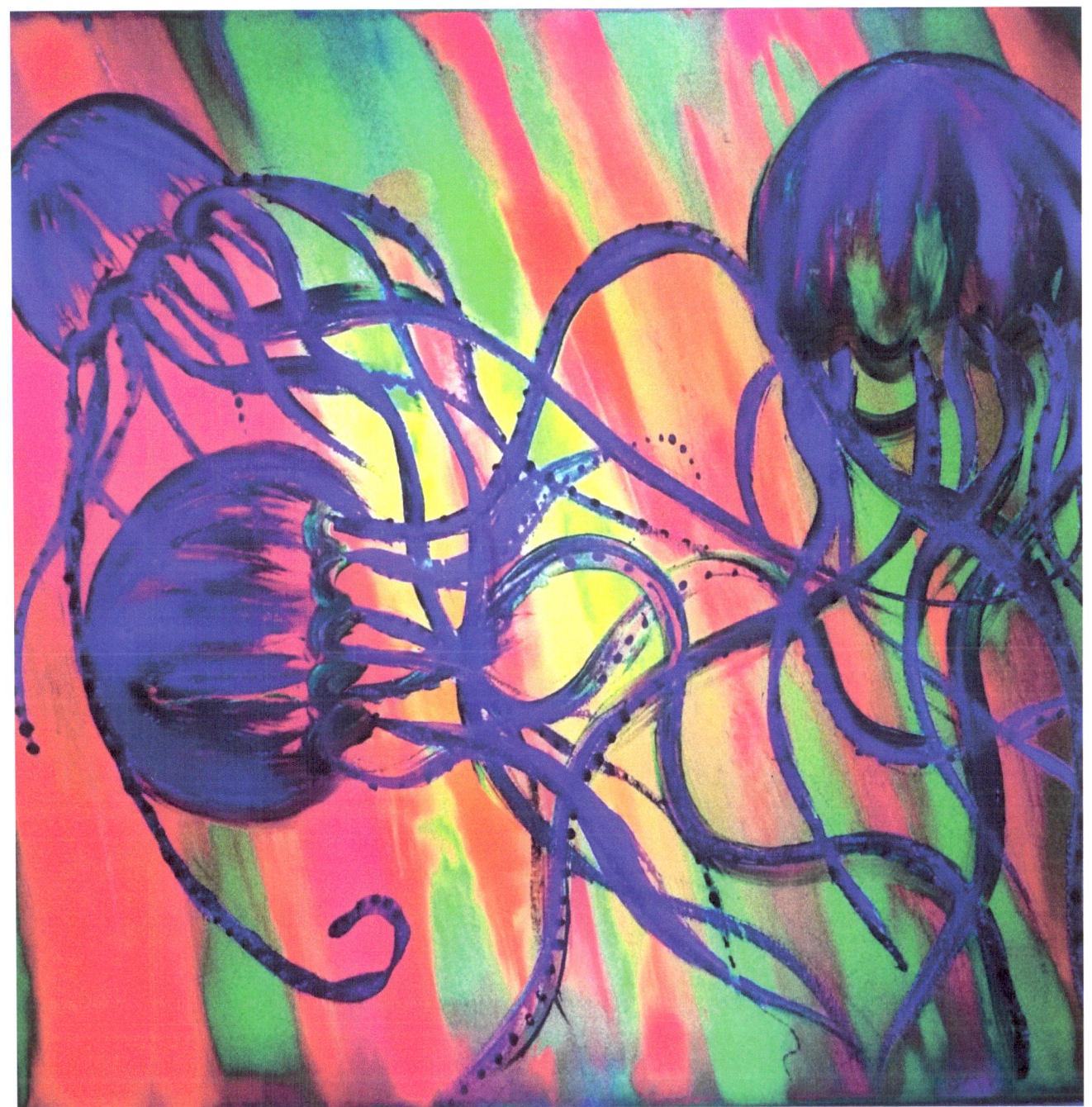

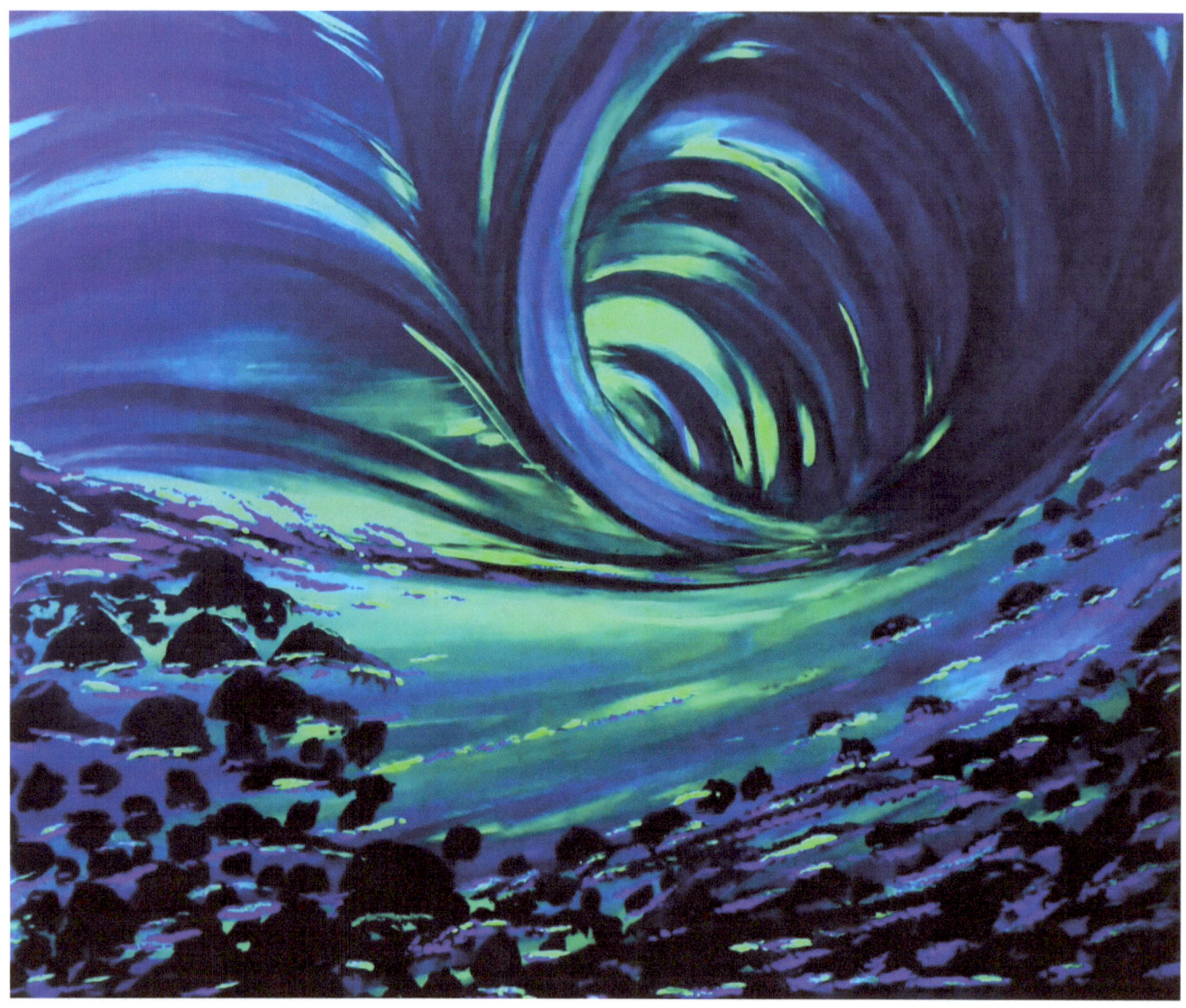

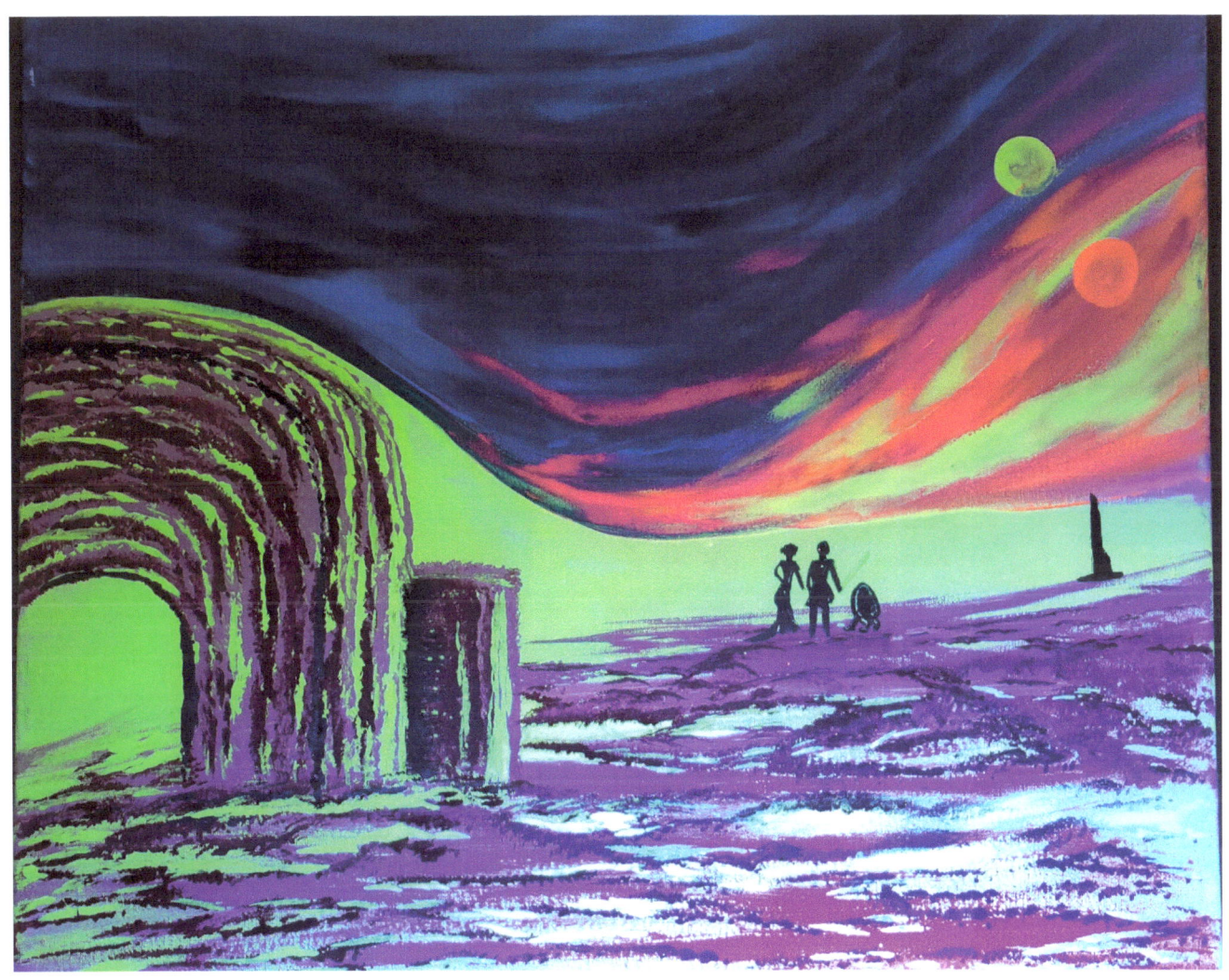

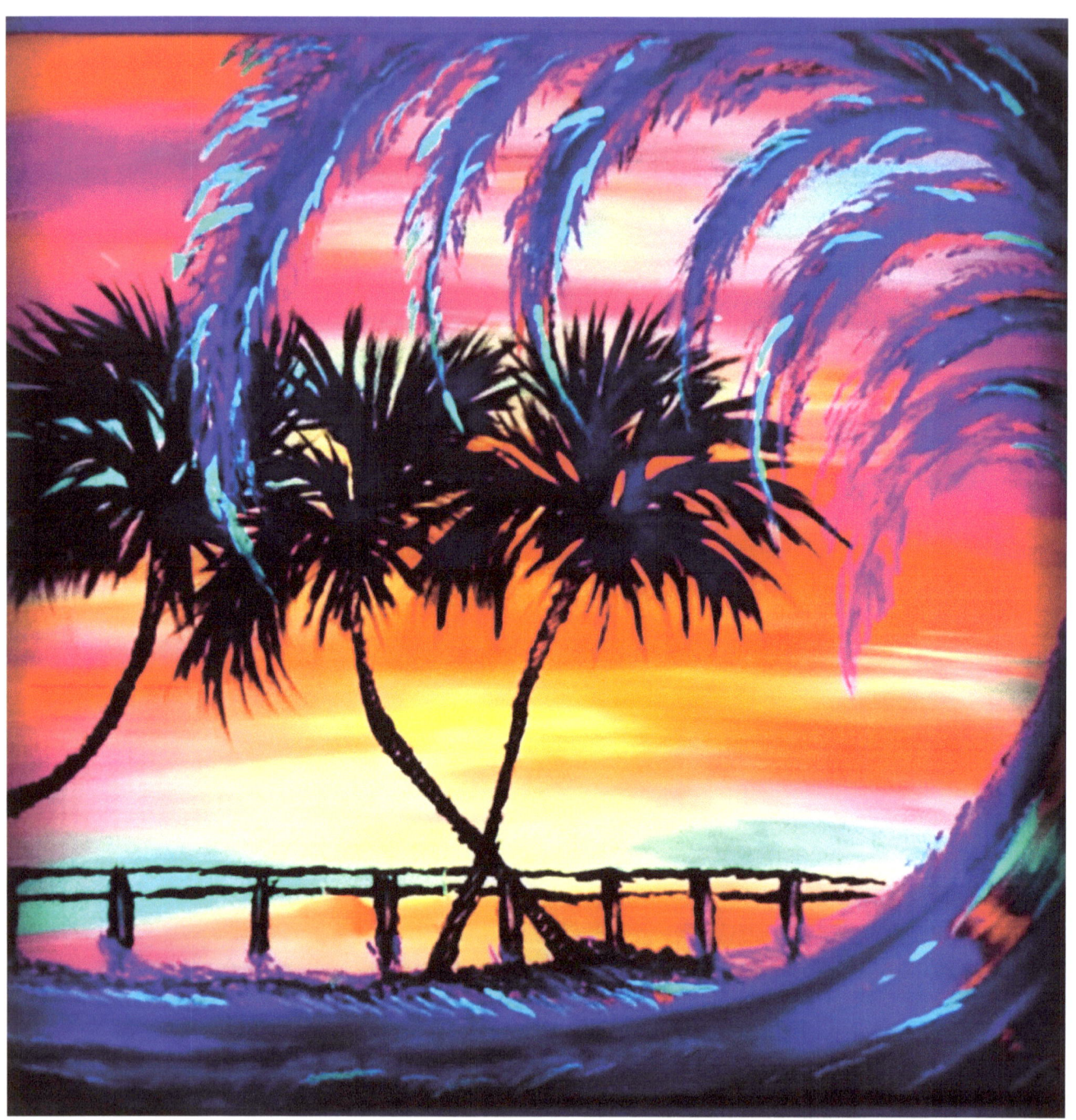

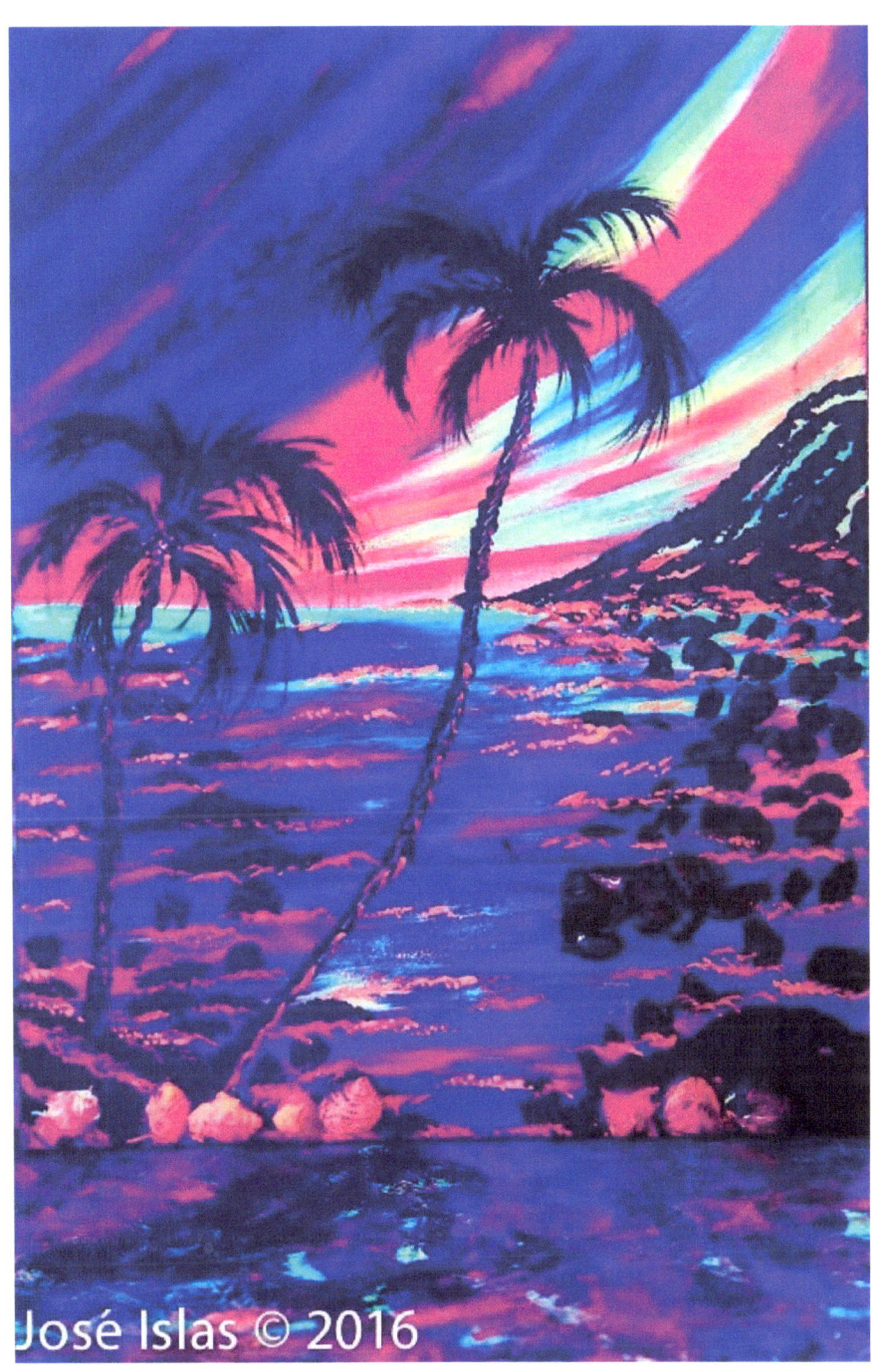

José Islas © 2016

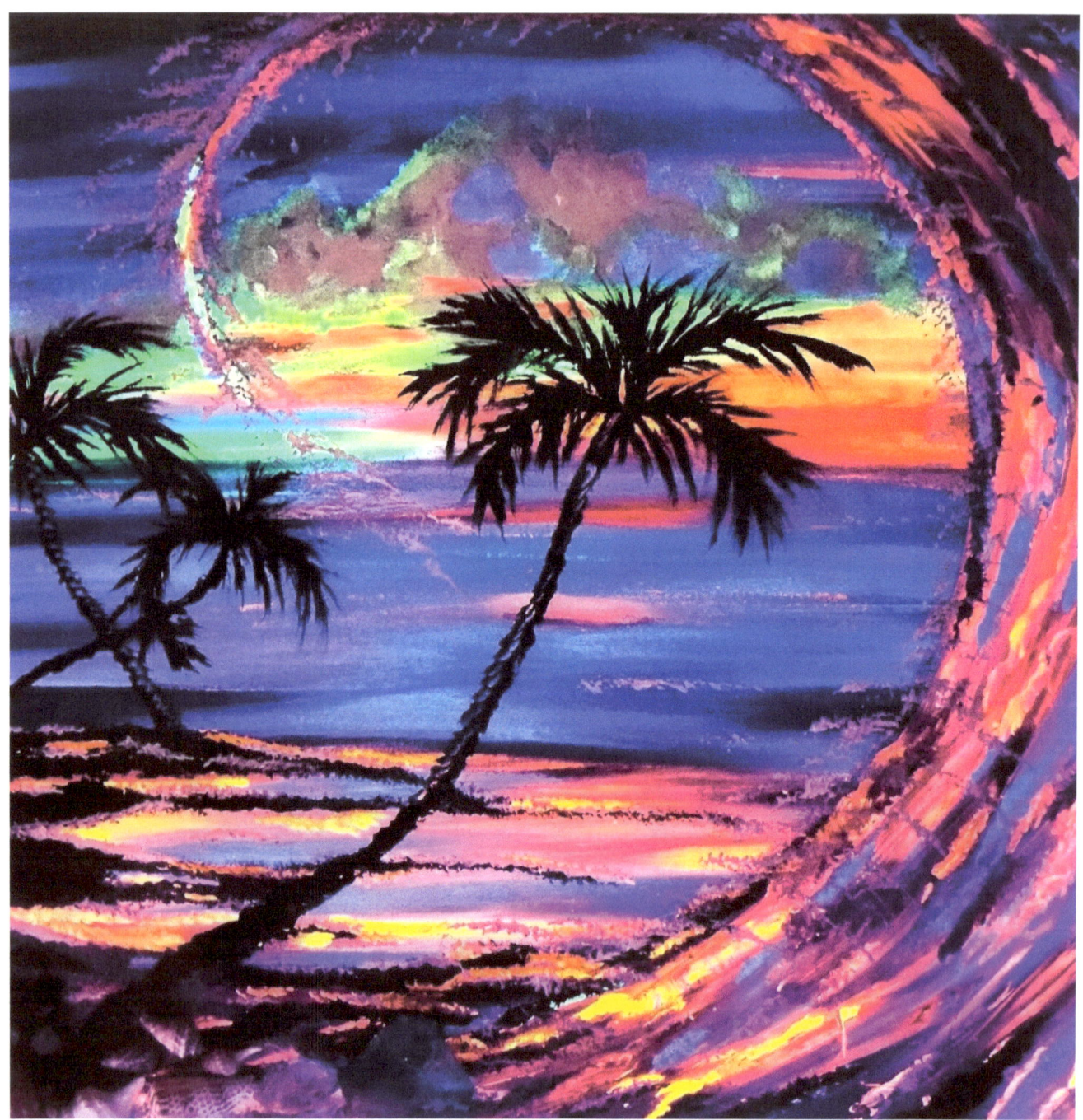

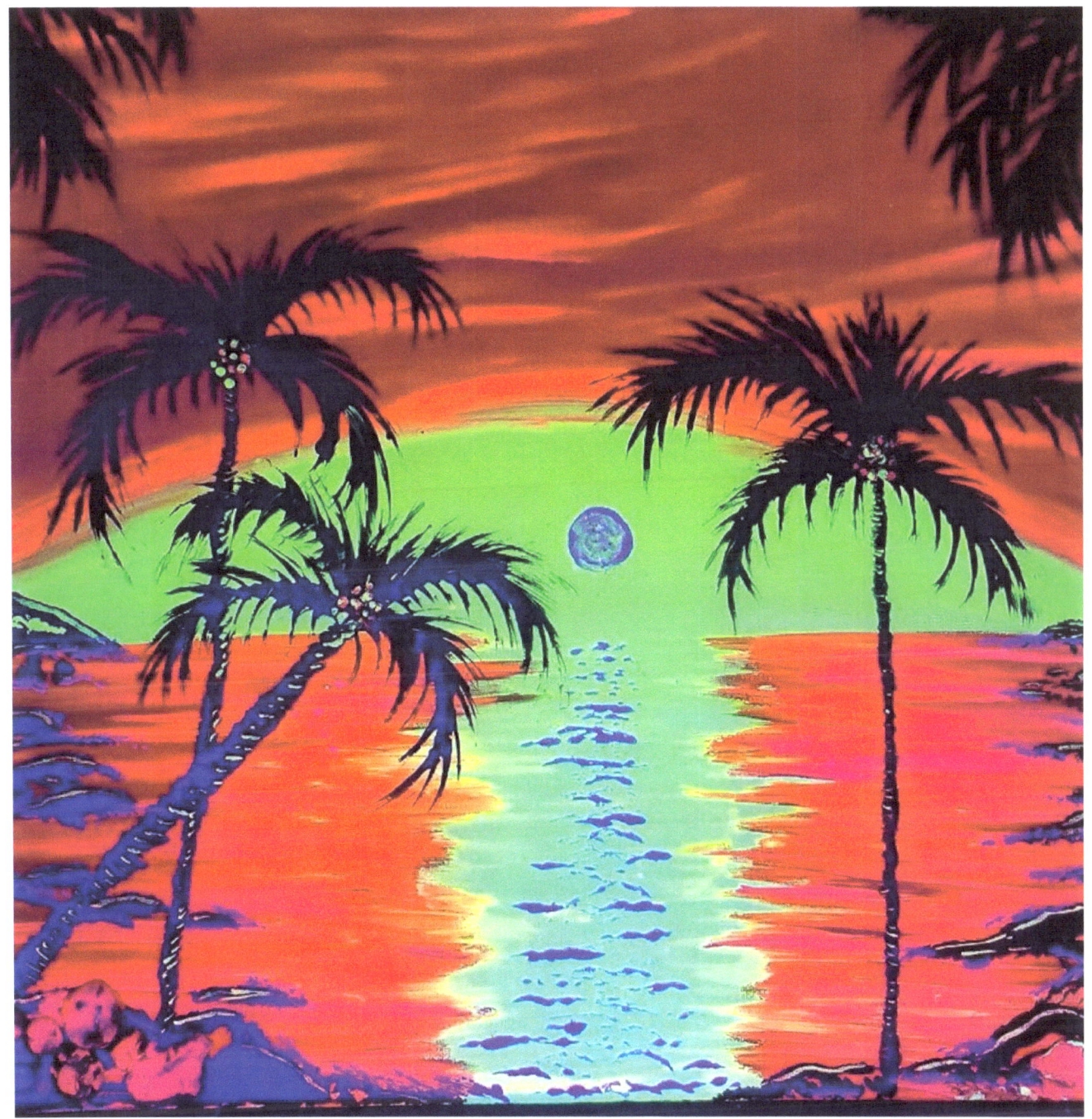

13

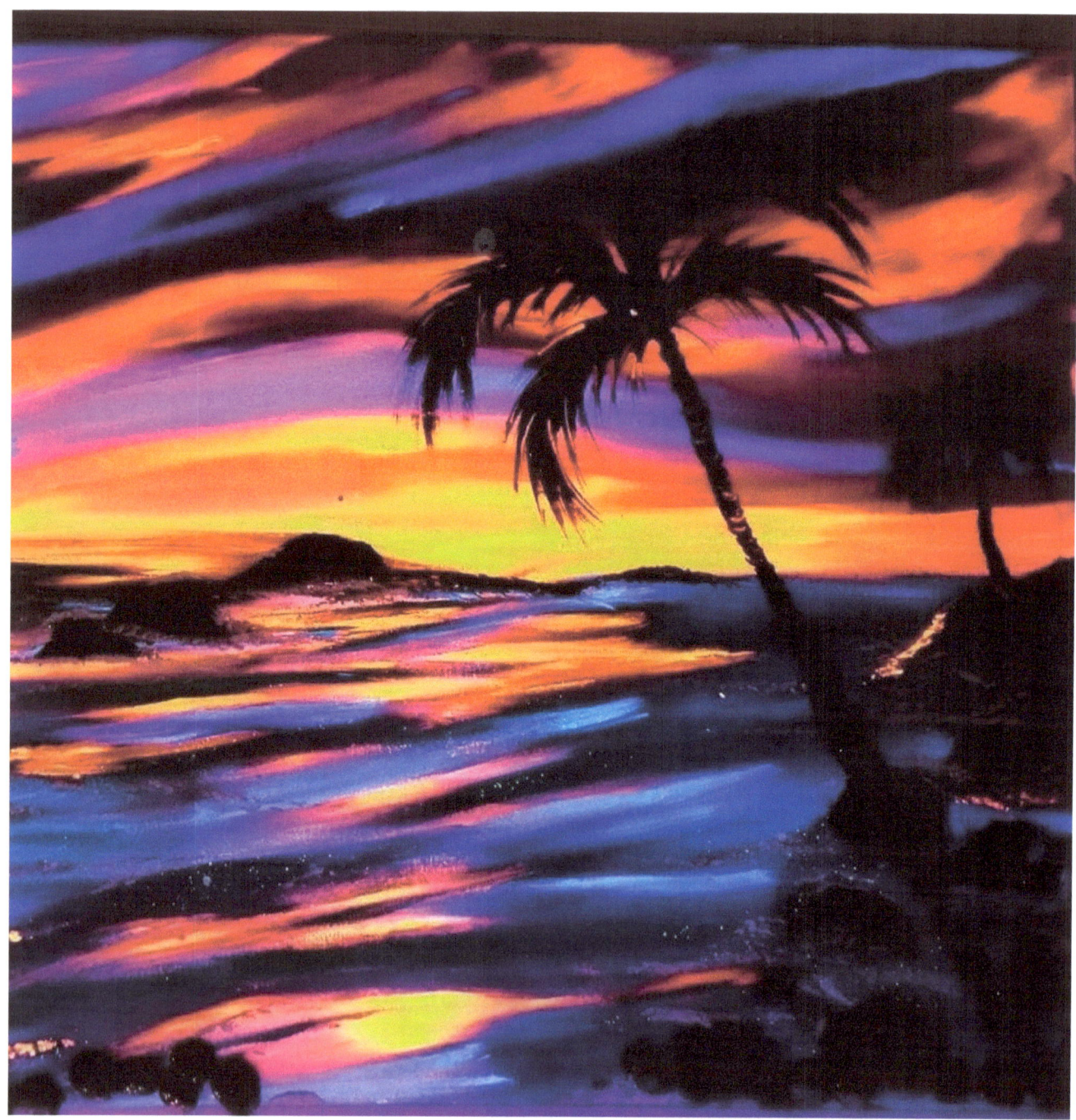

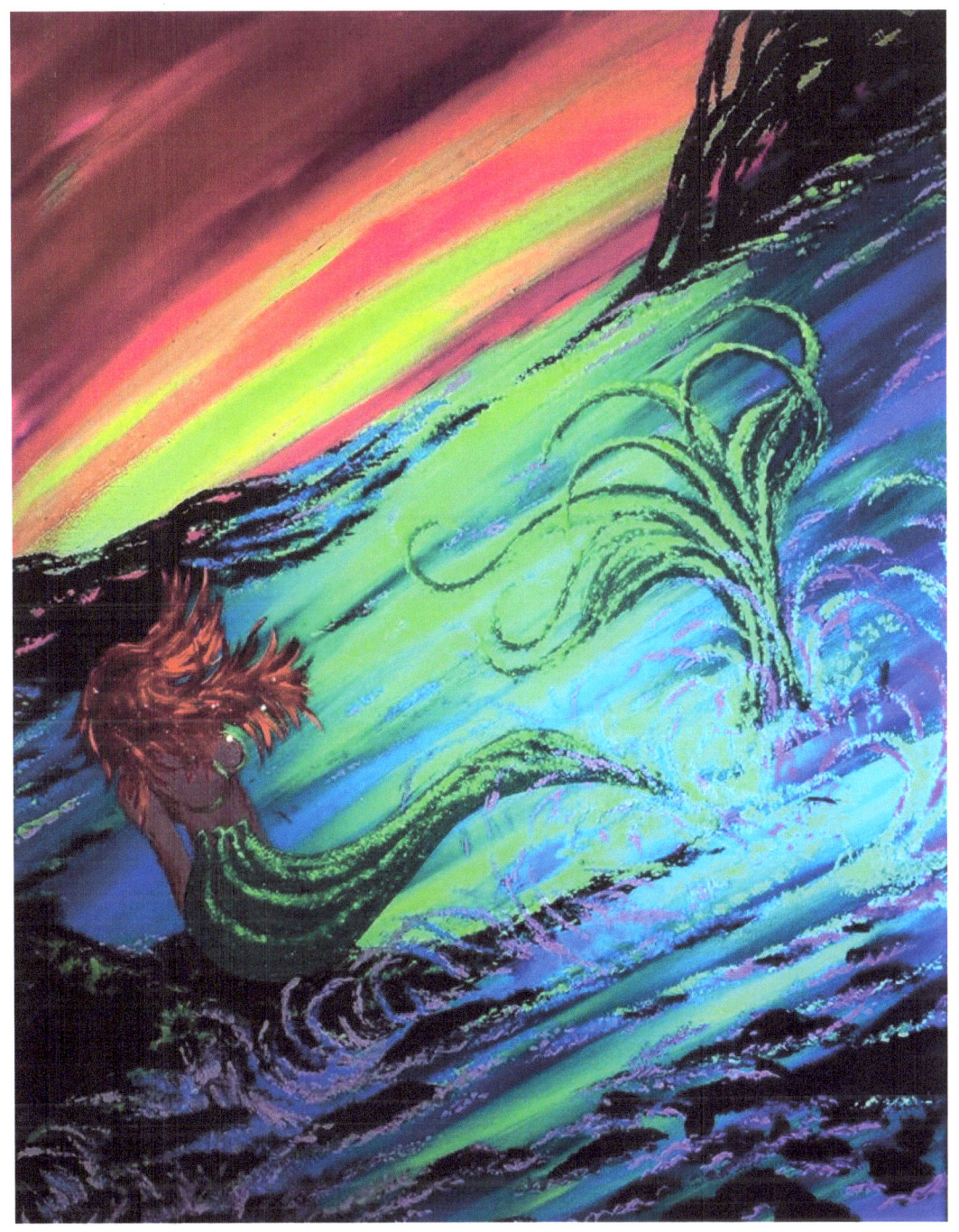

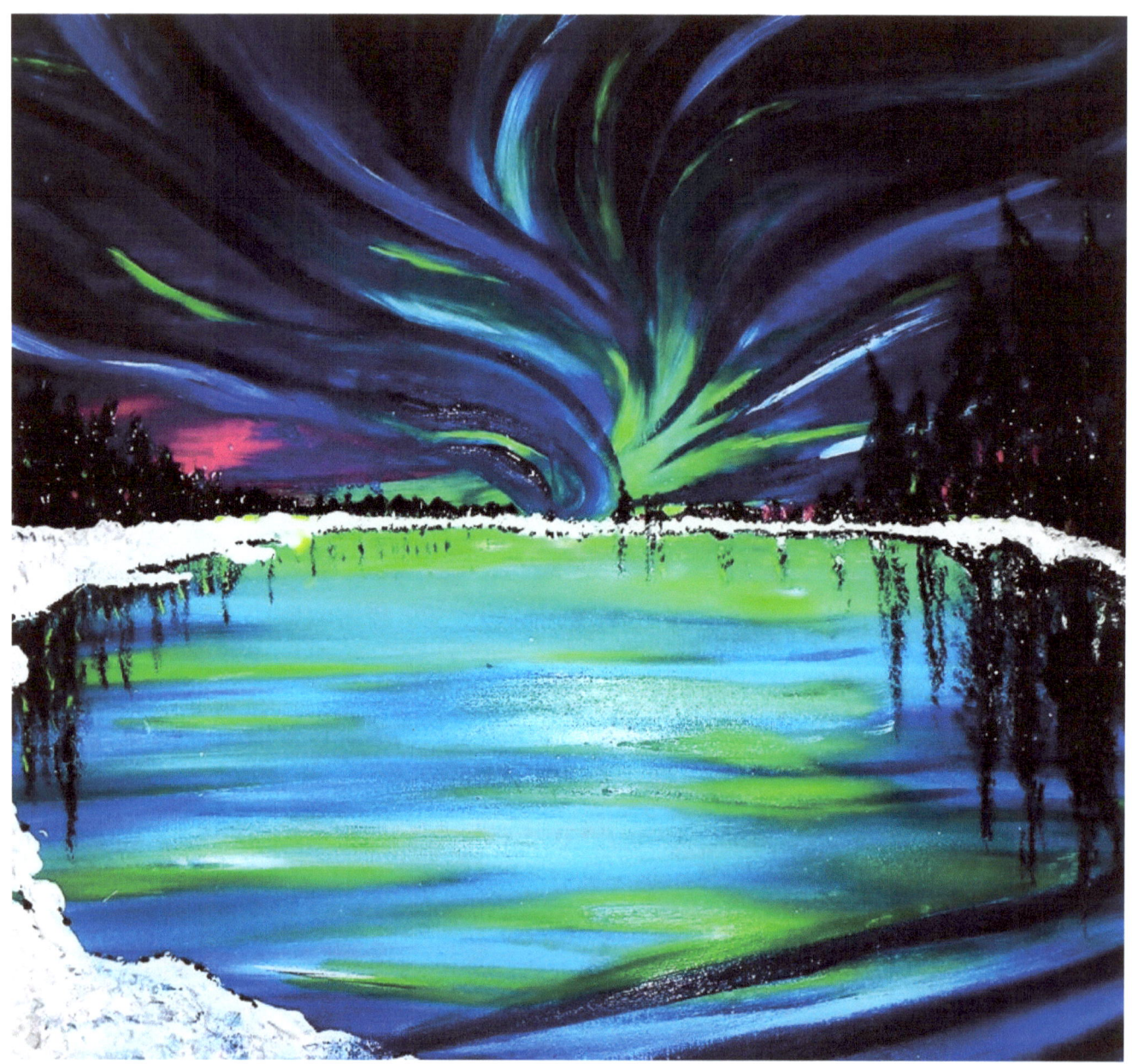

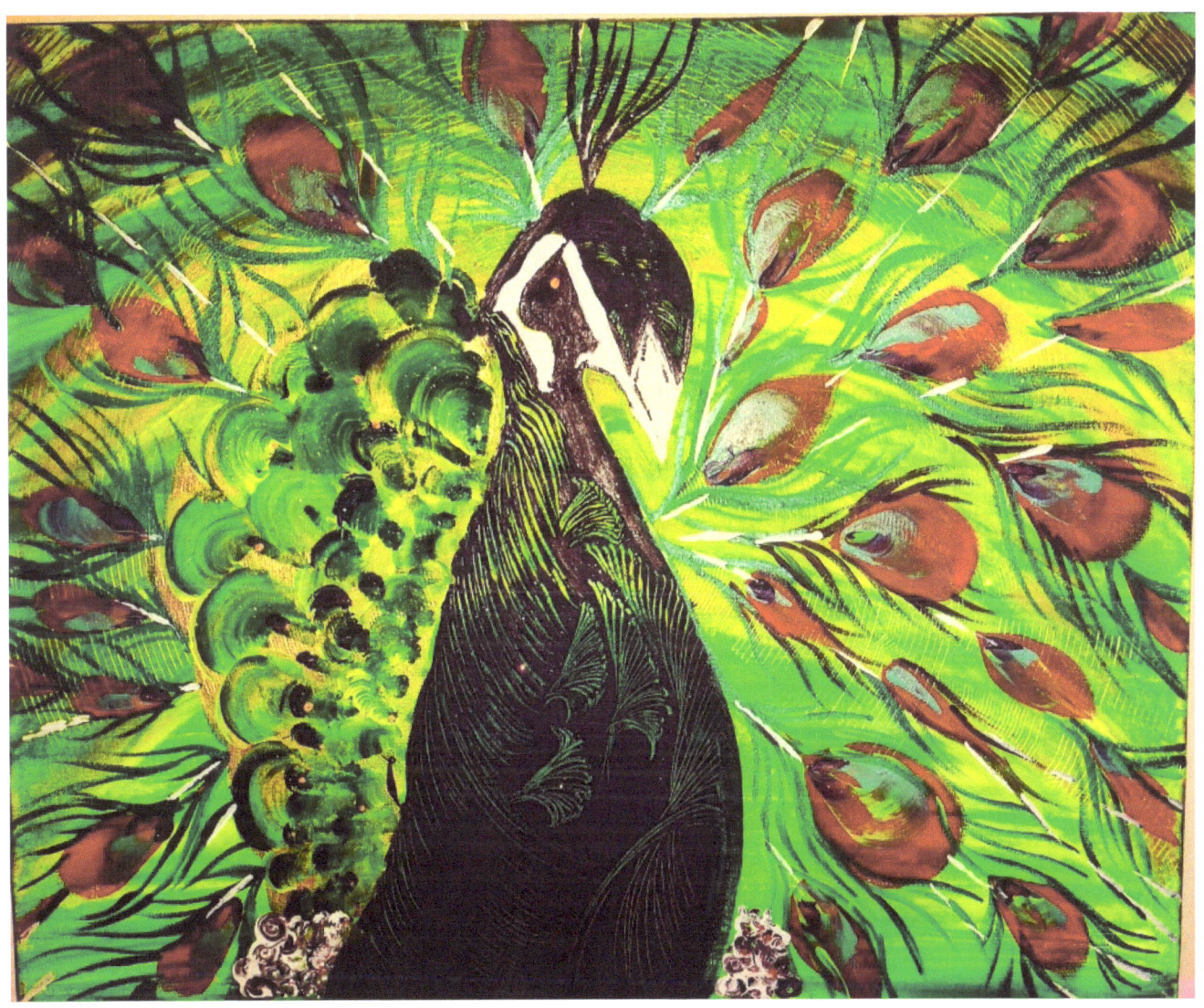

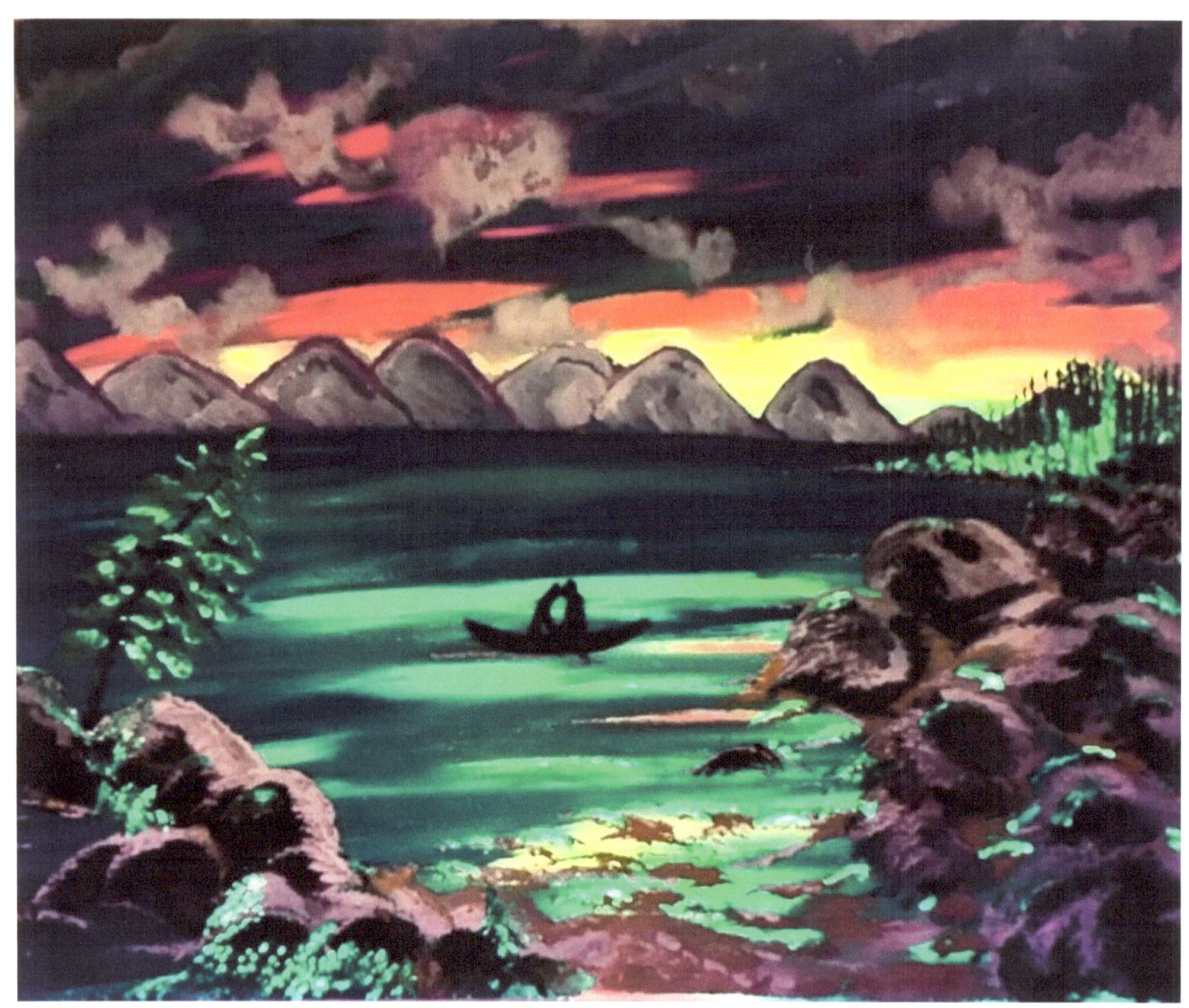

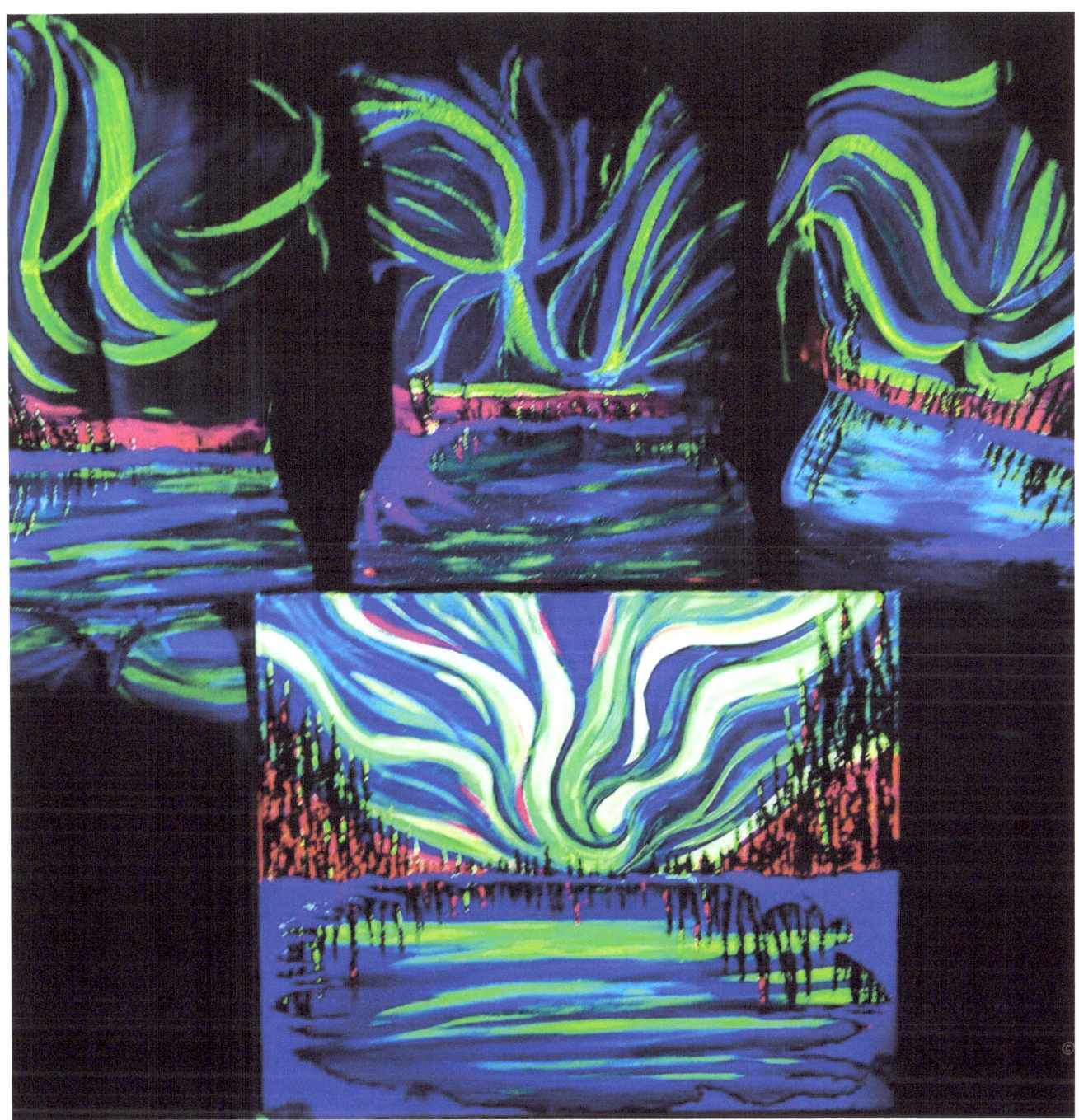

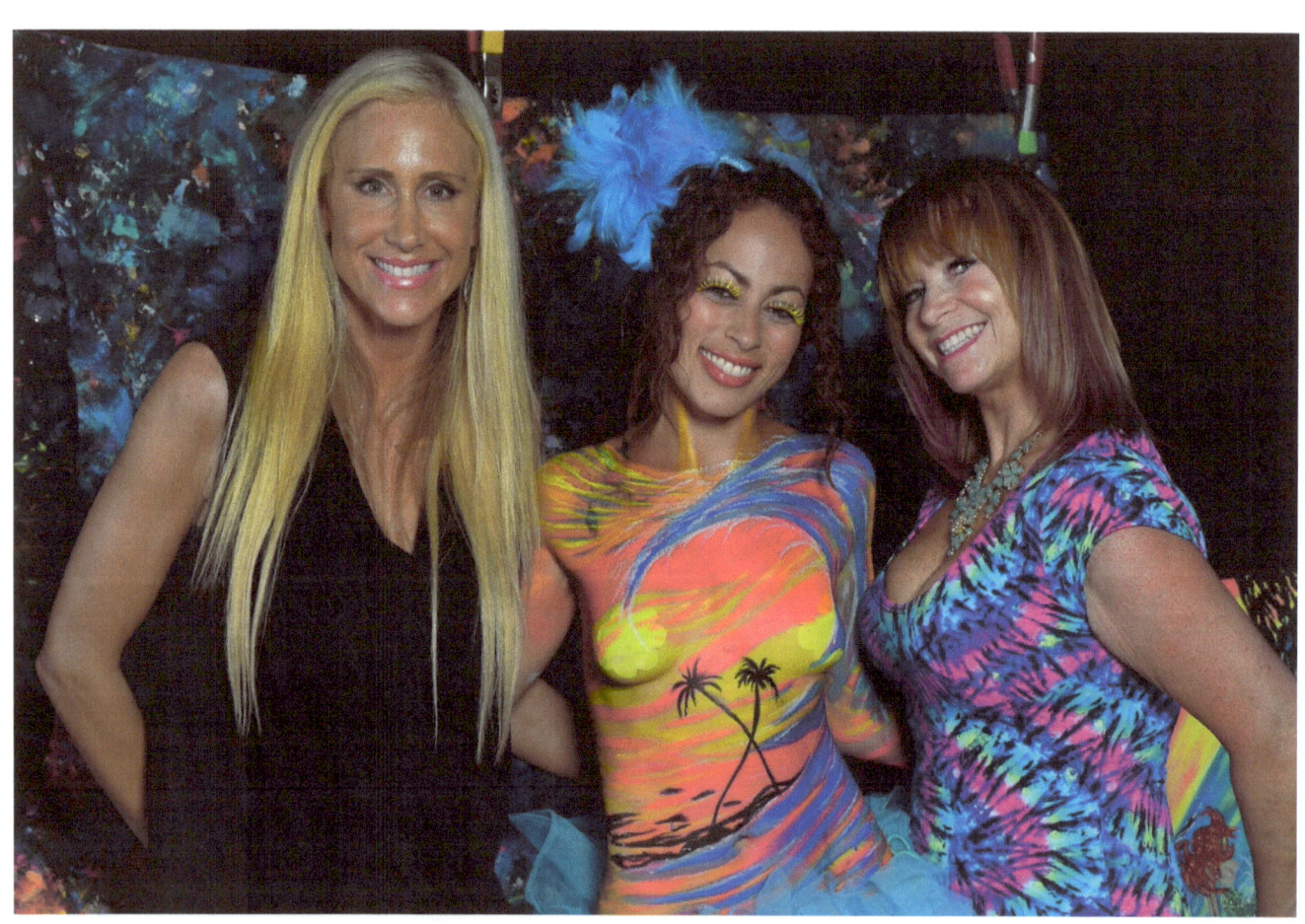

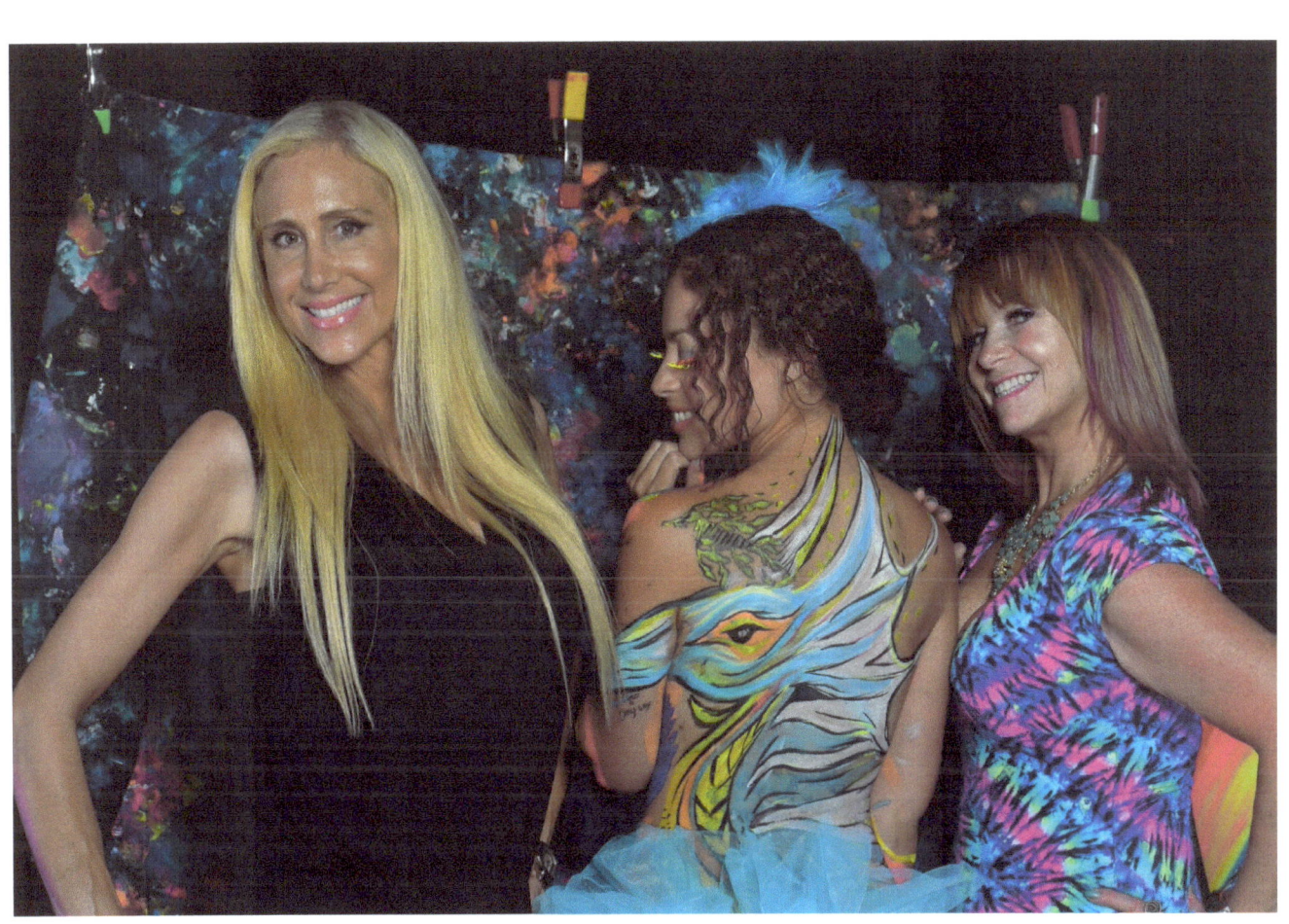

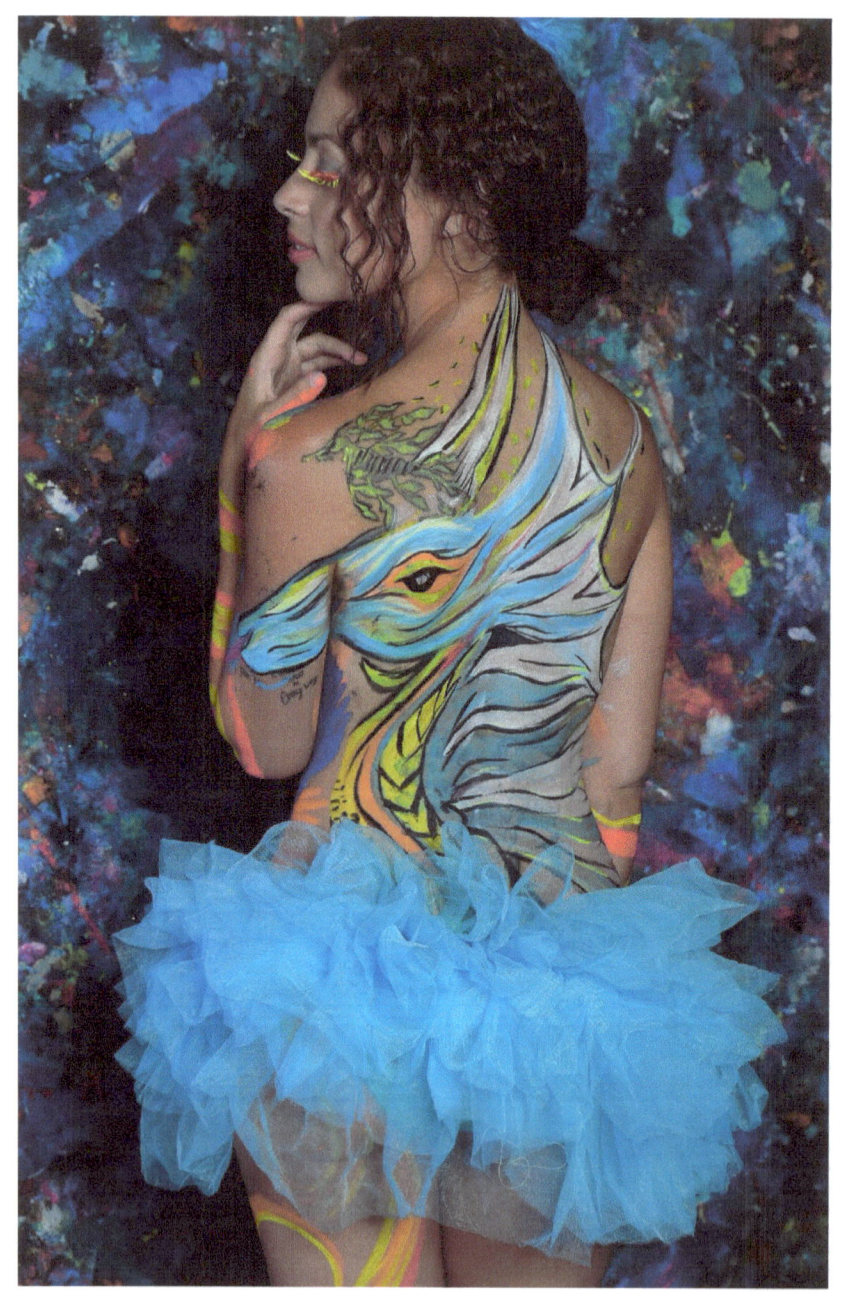

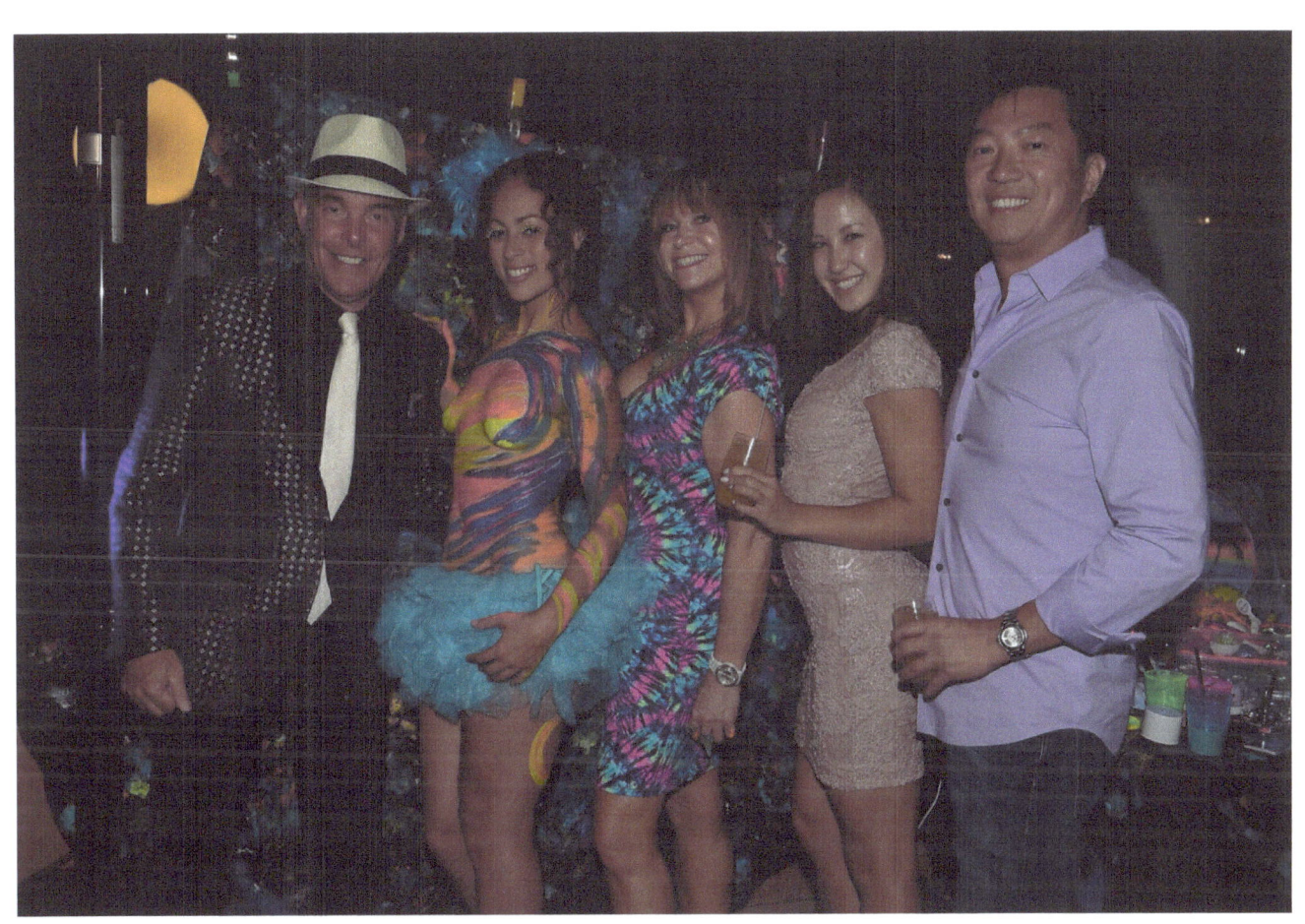

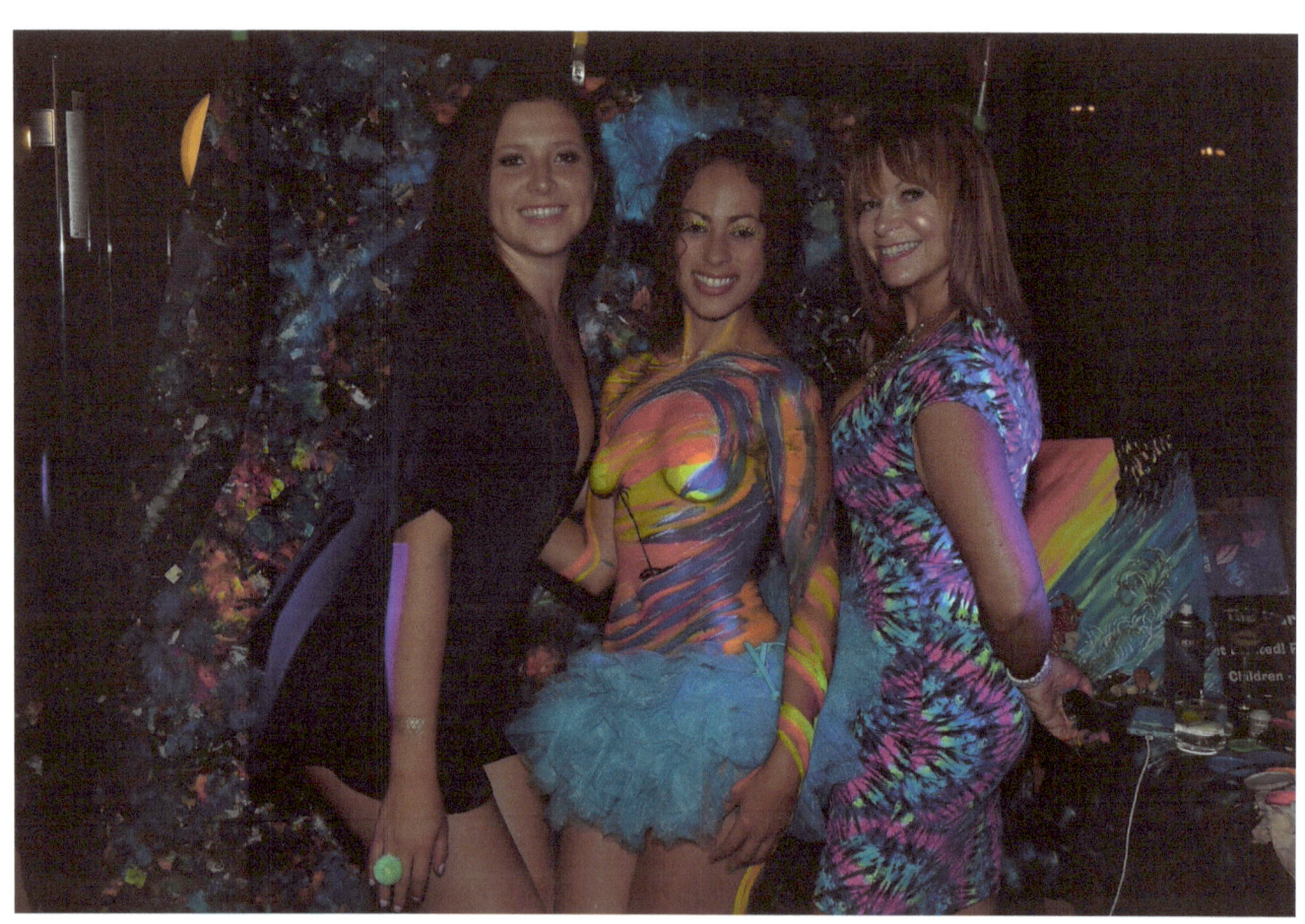

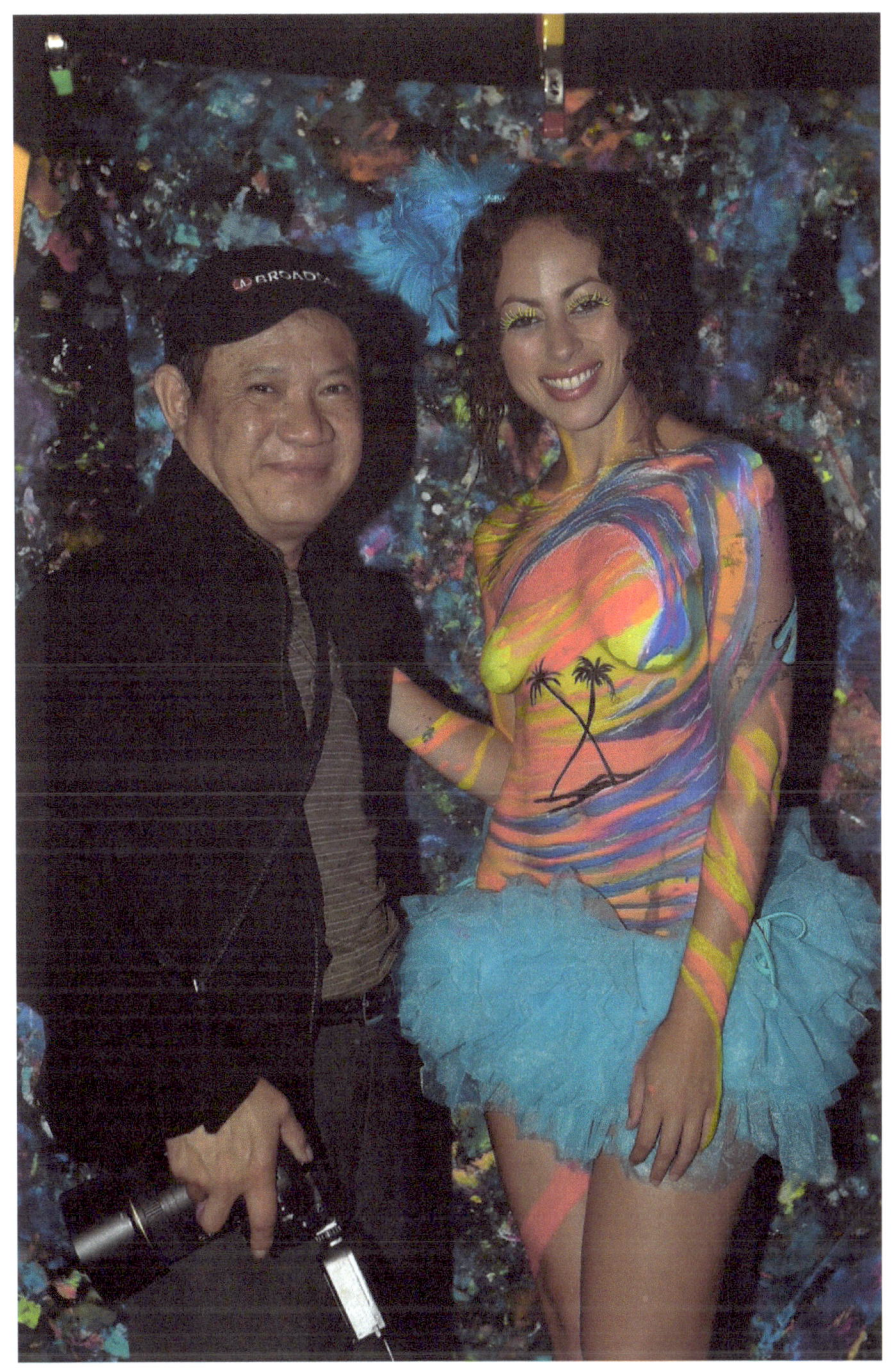

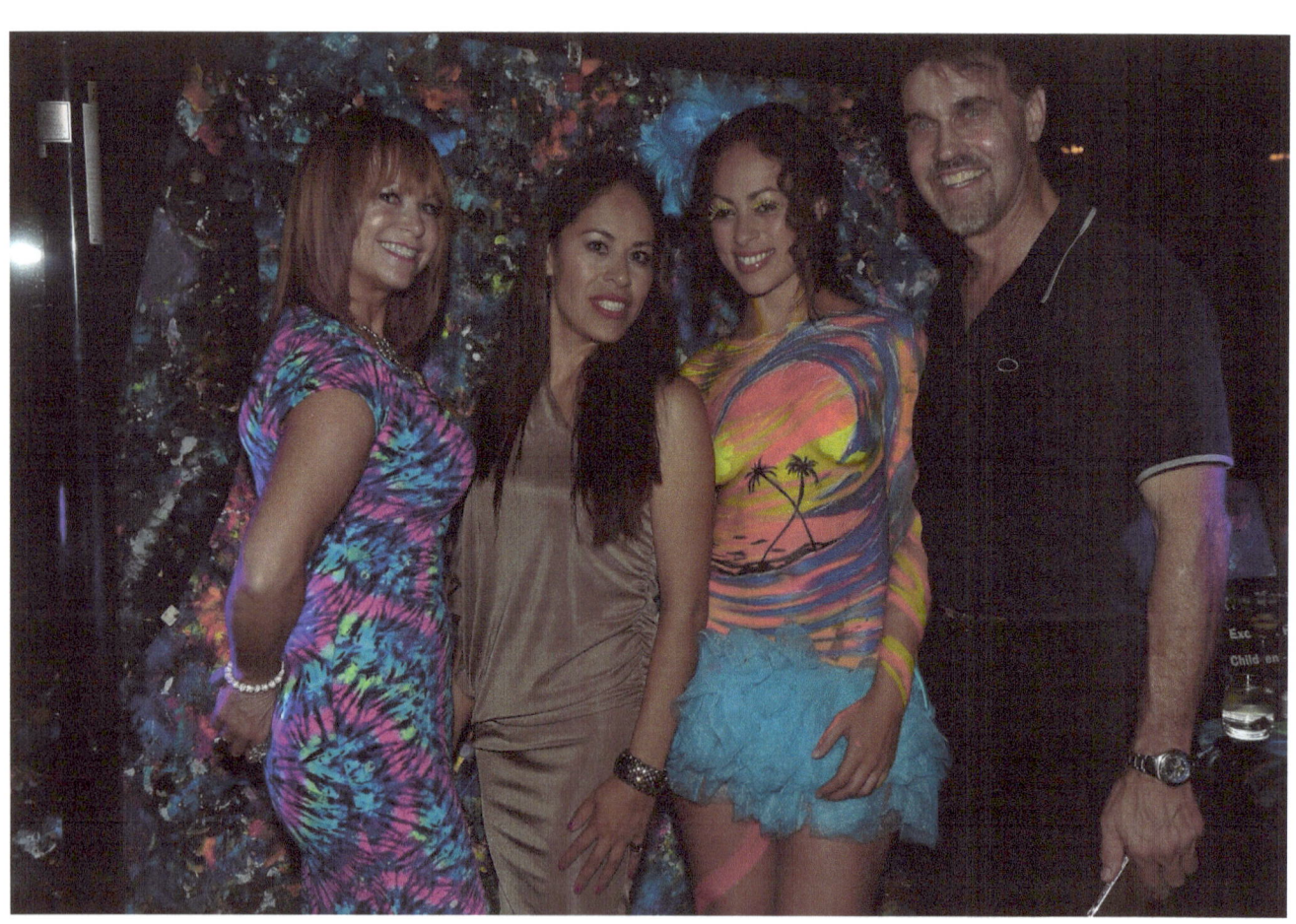

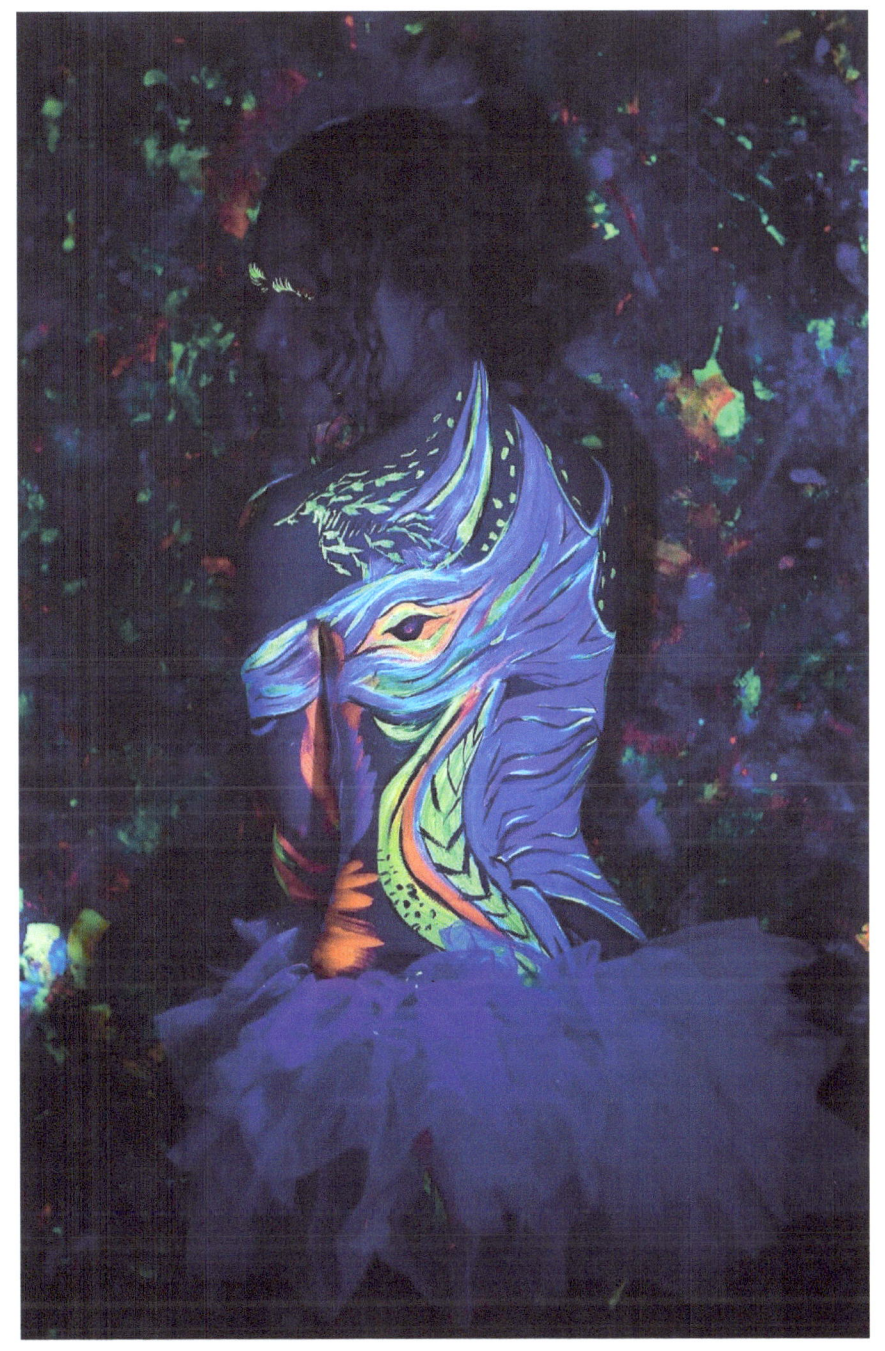

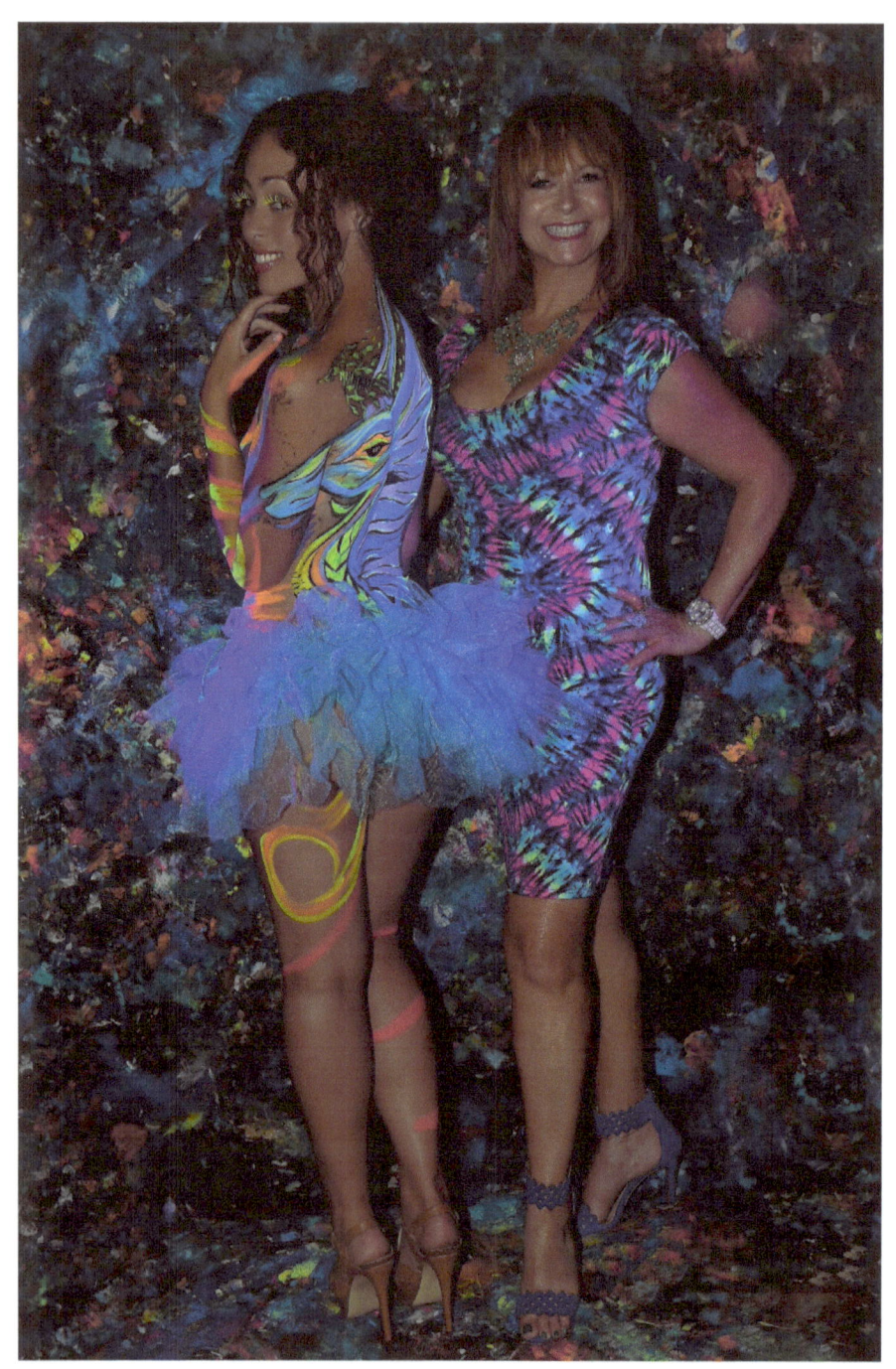

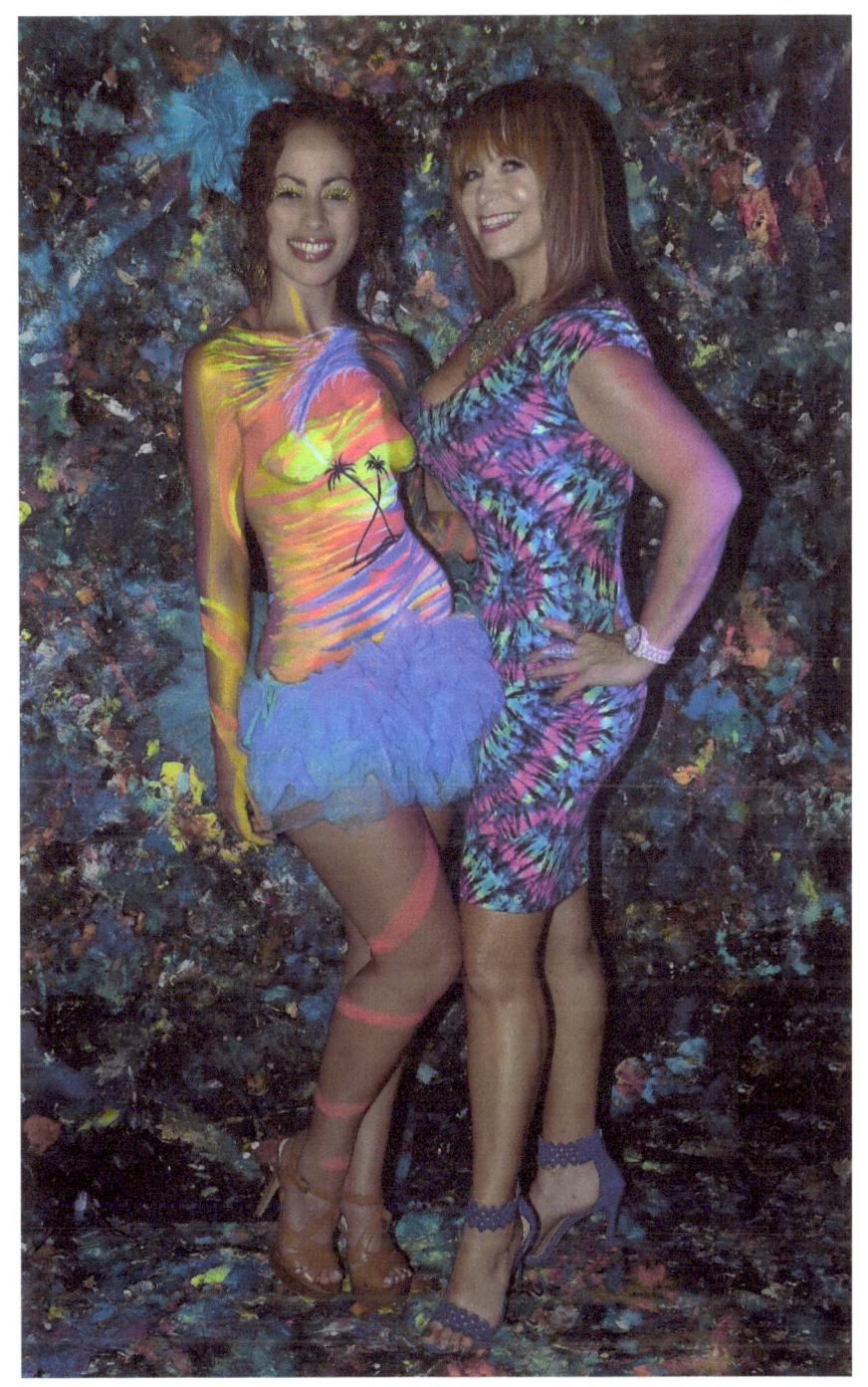

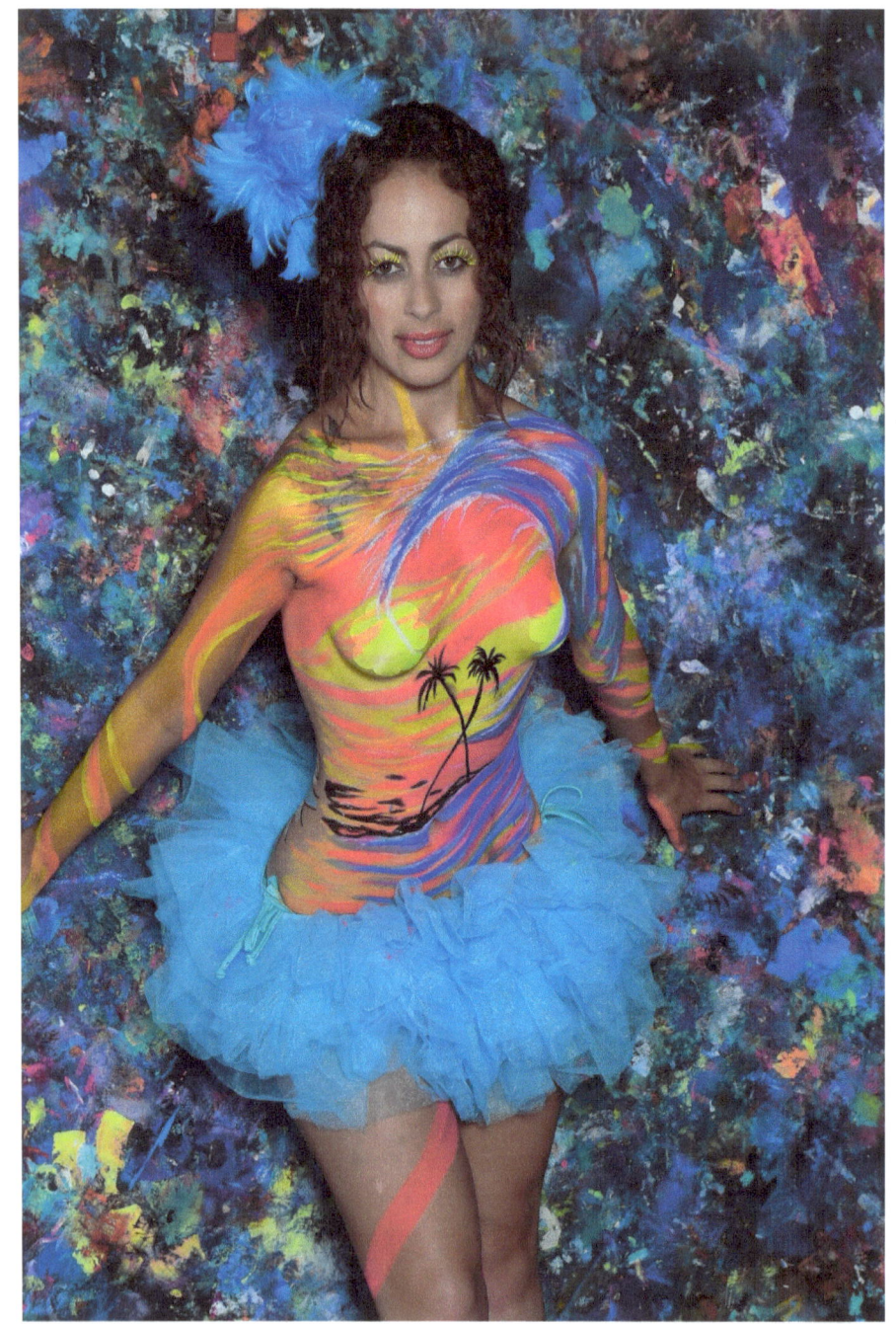

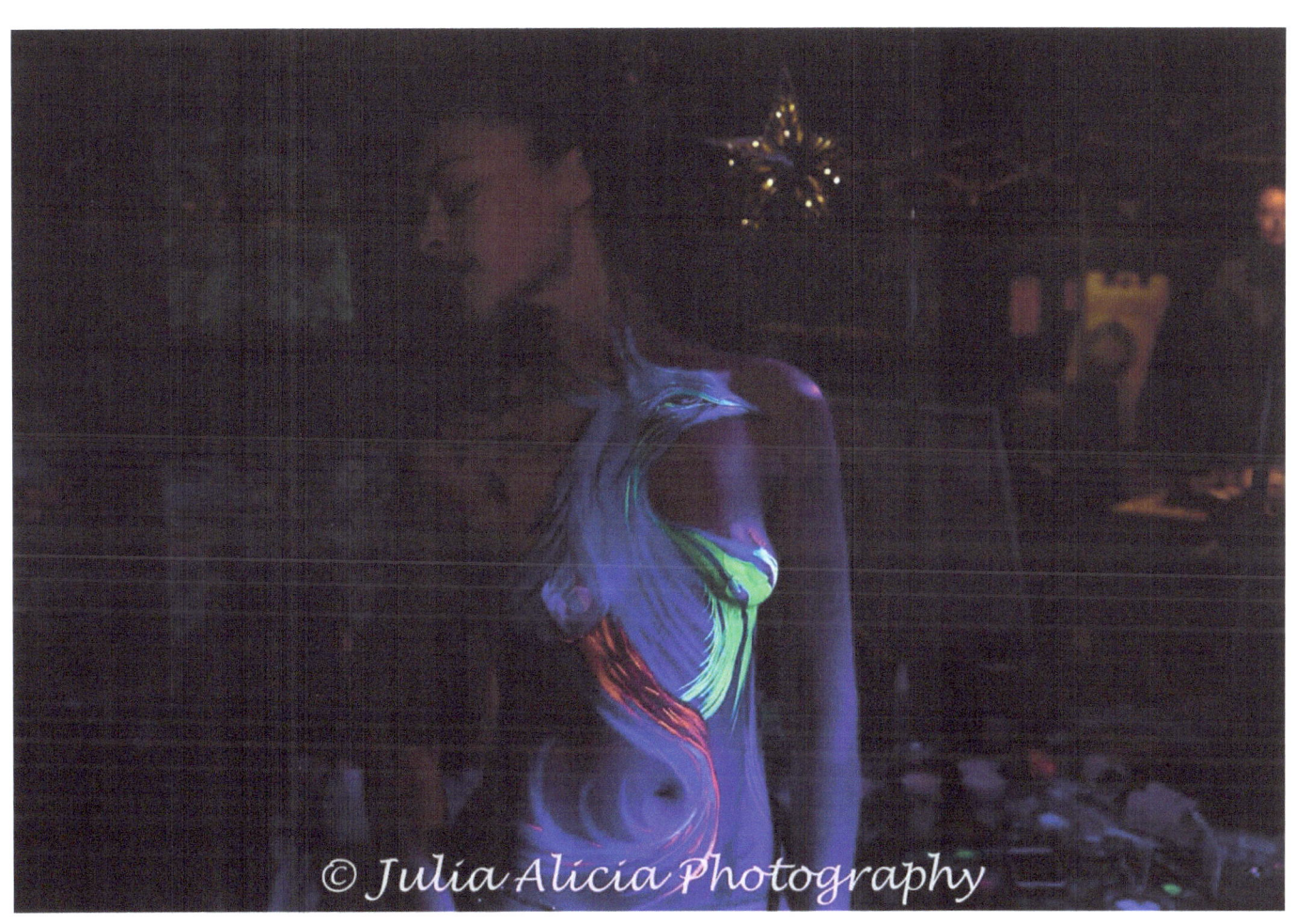

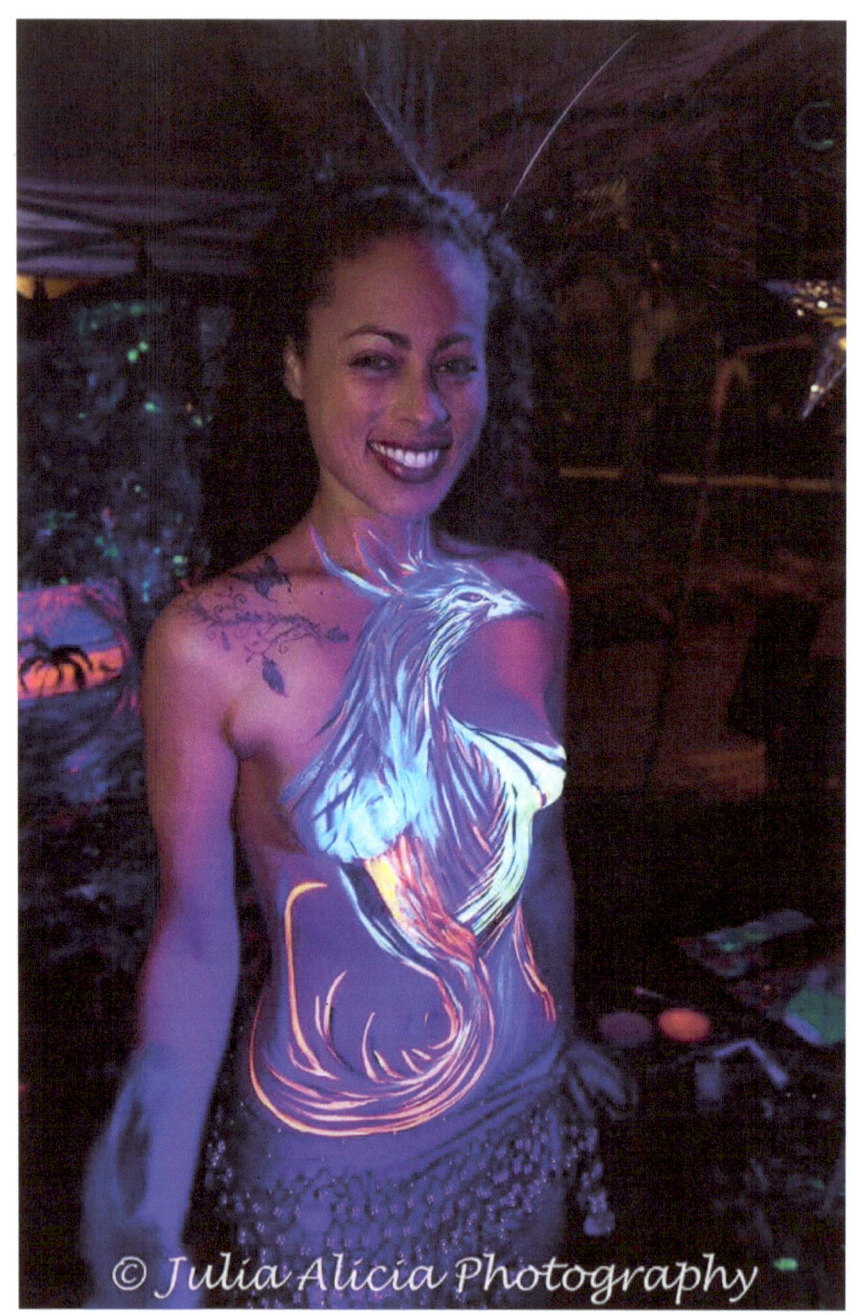

© Julia Alicia Photography

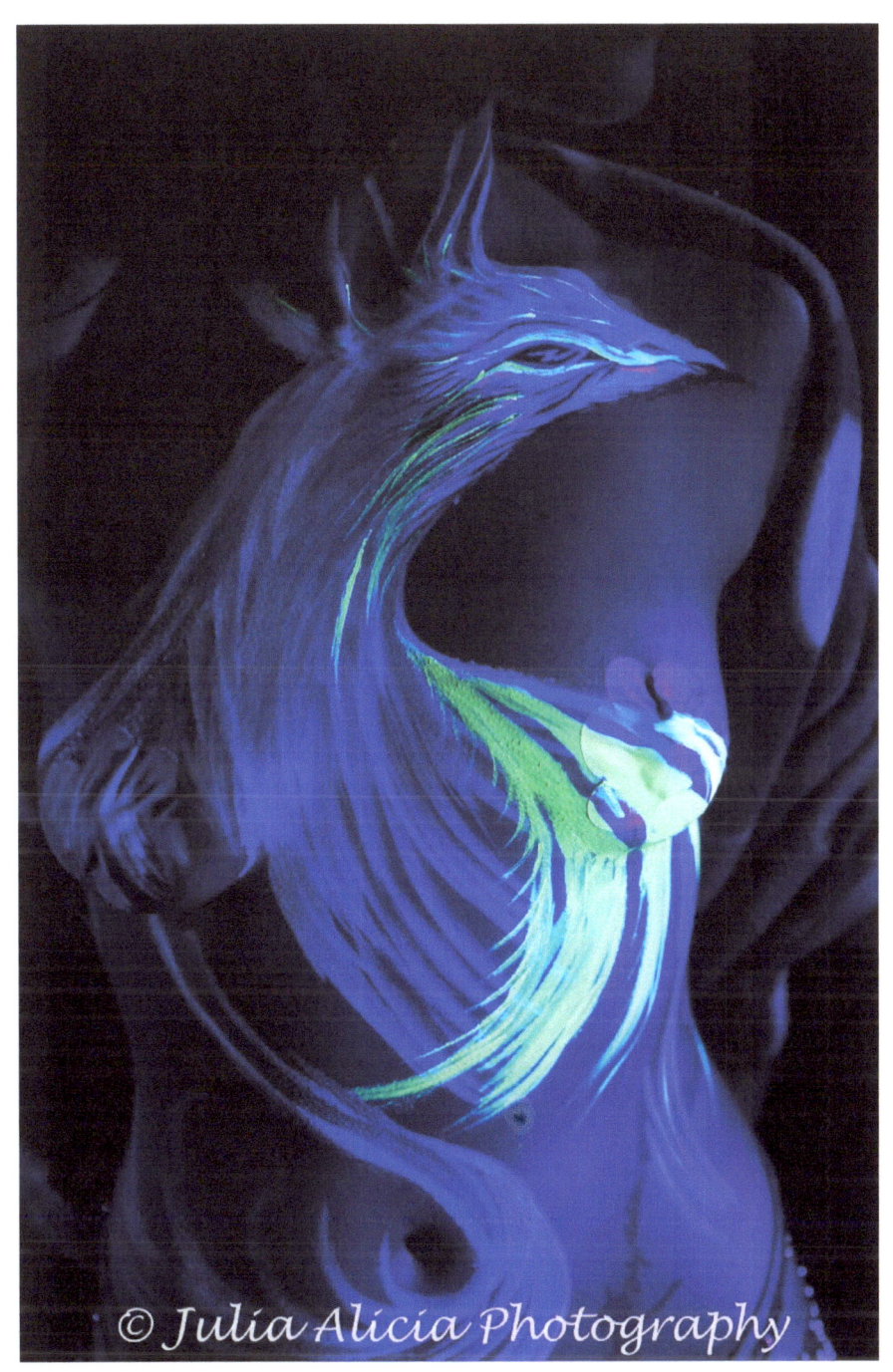

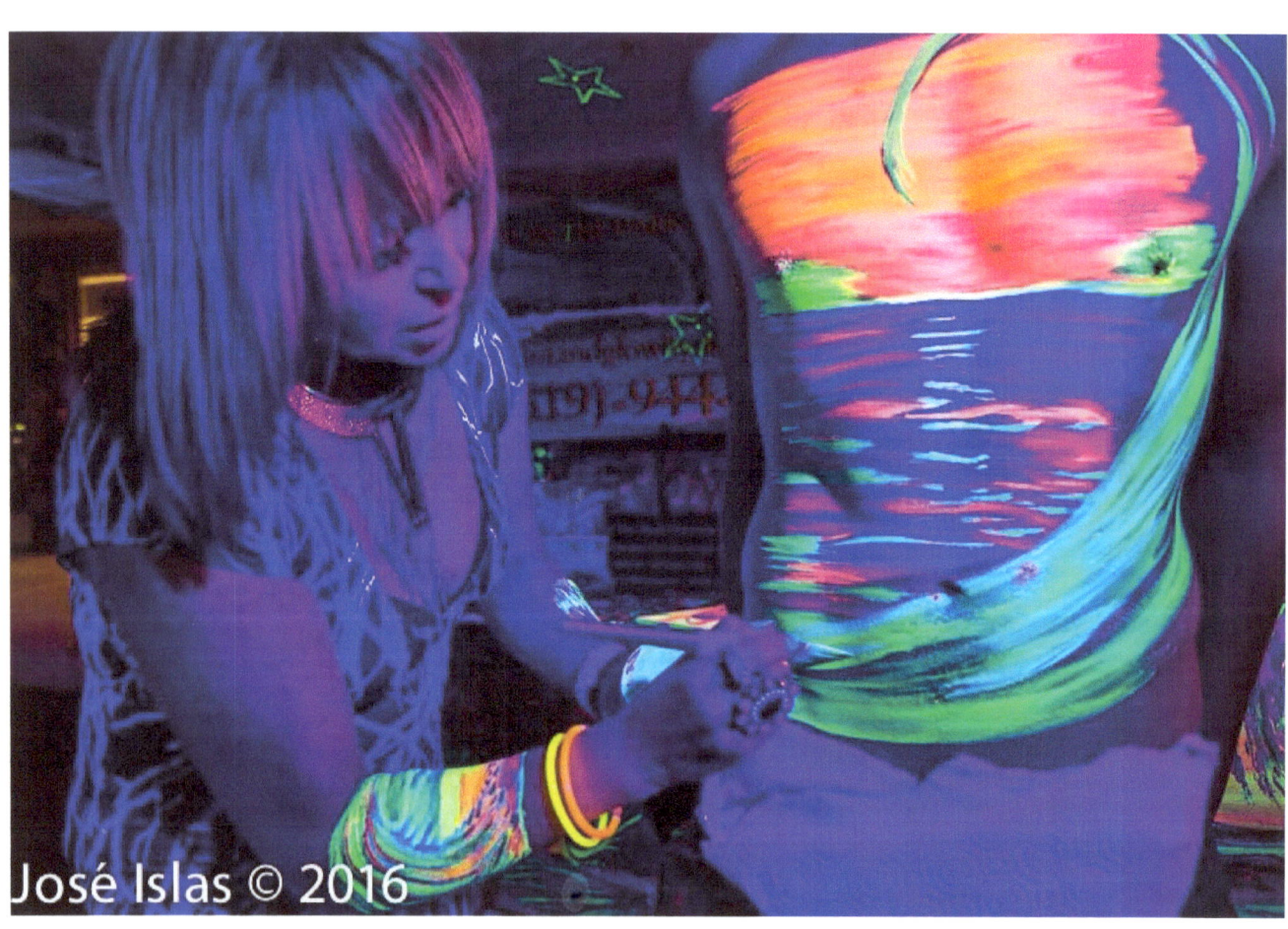

José Islas © 2016

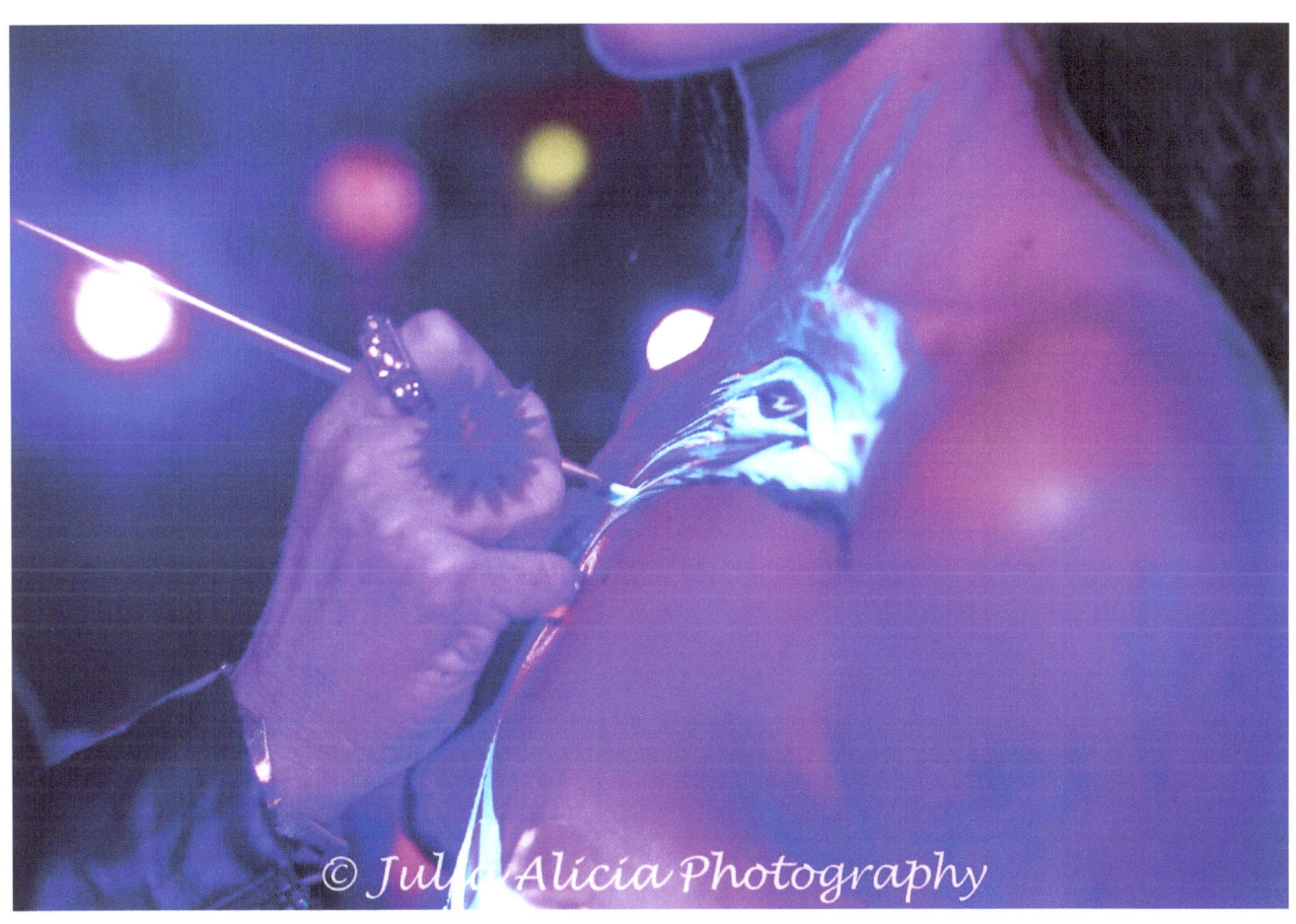

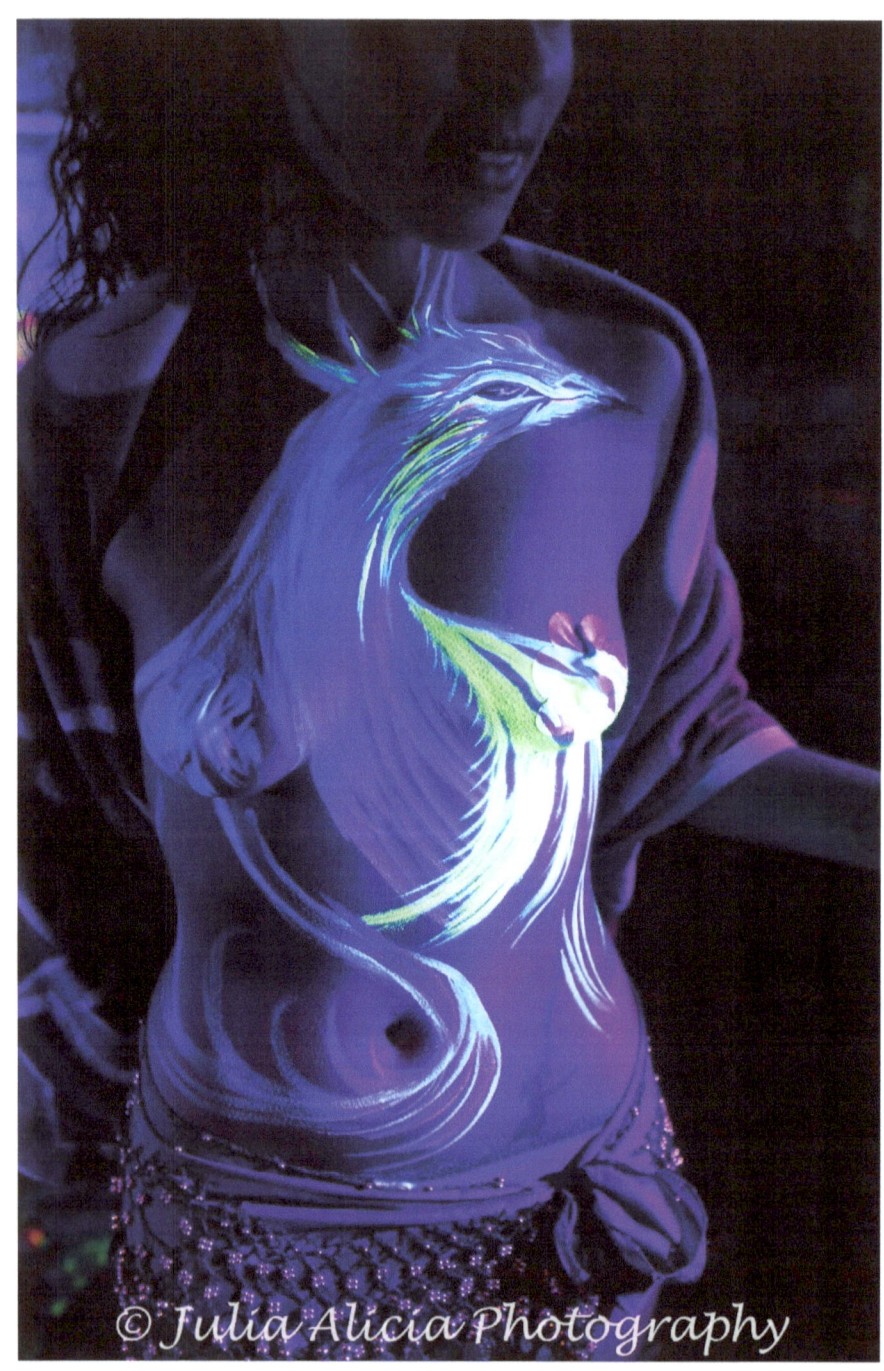

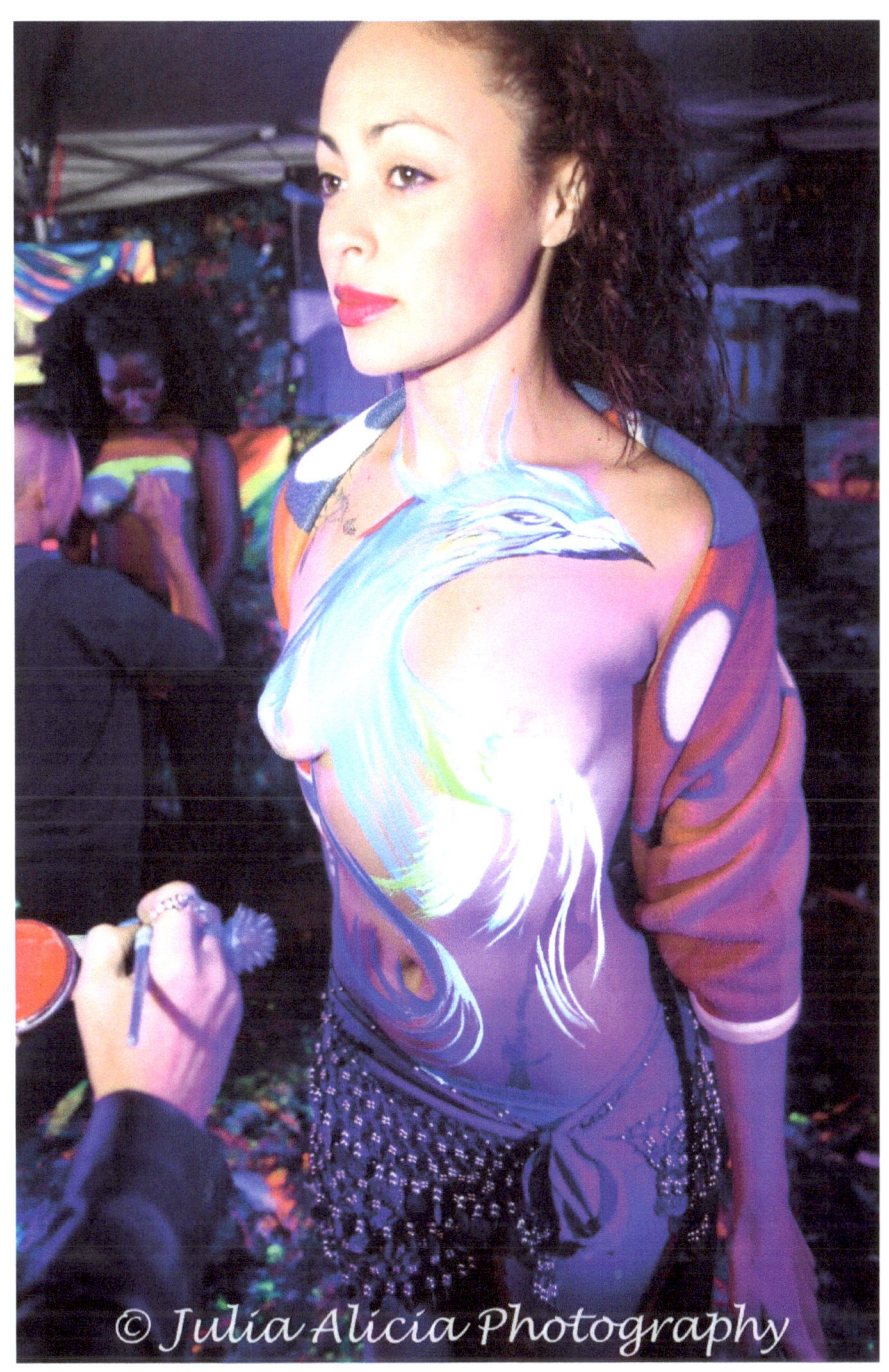

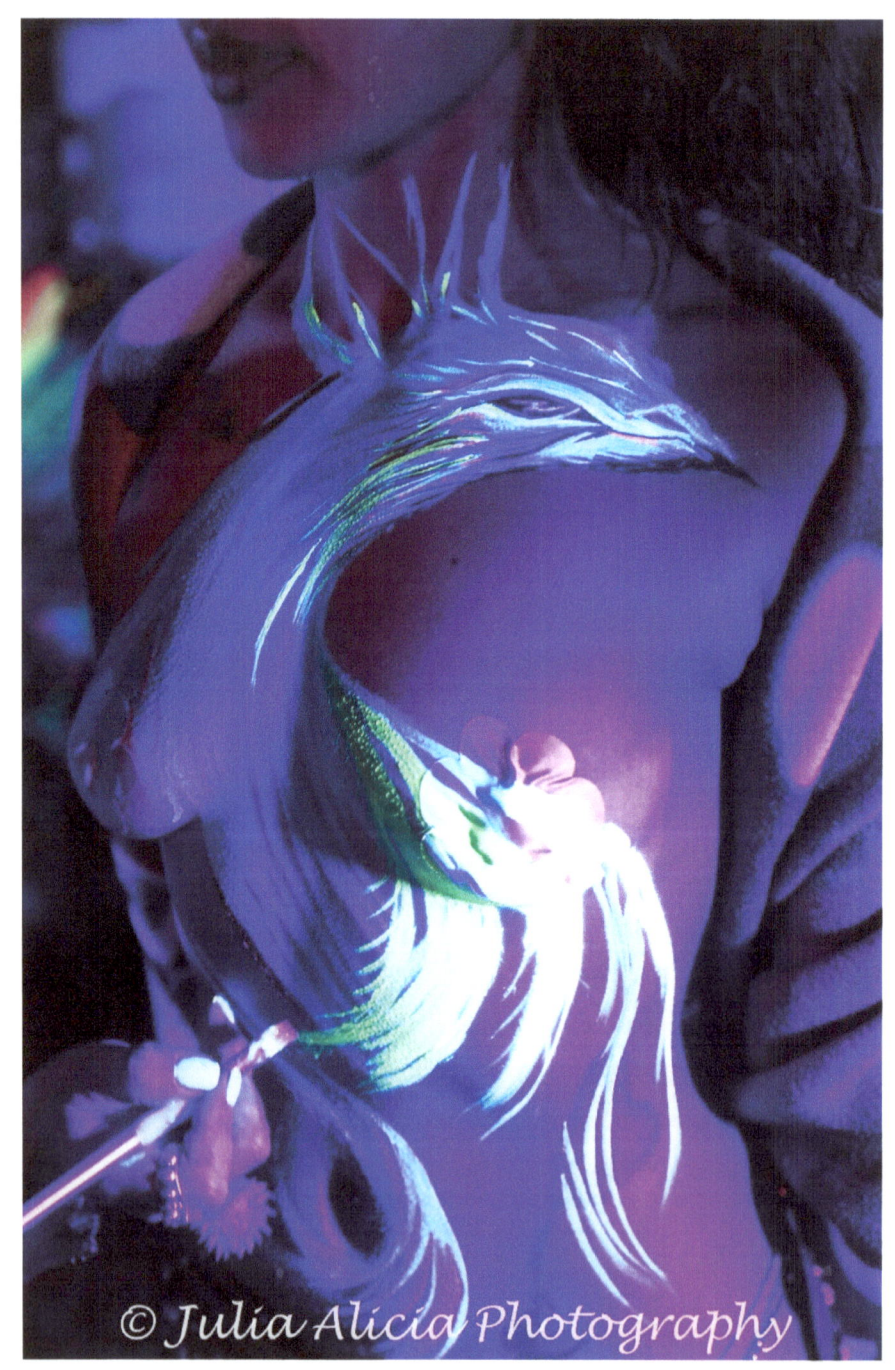

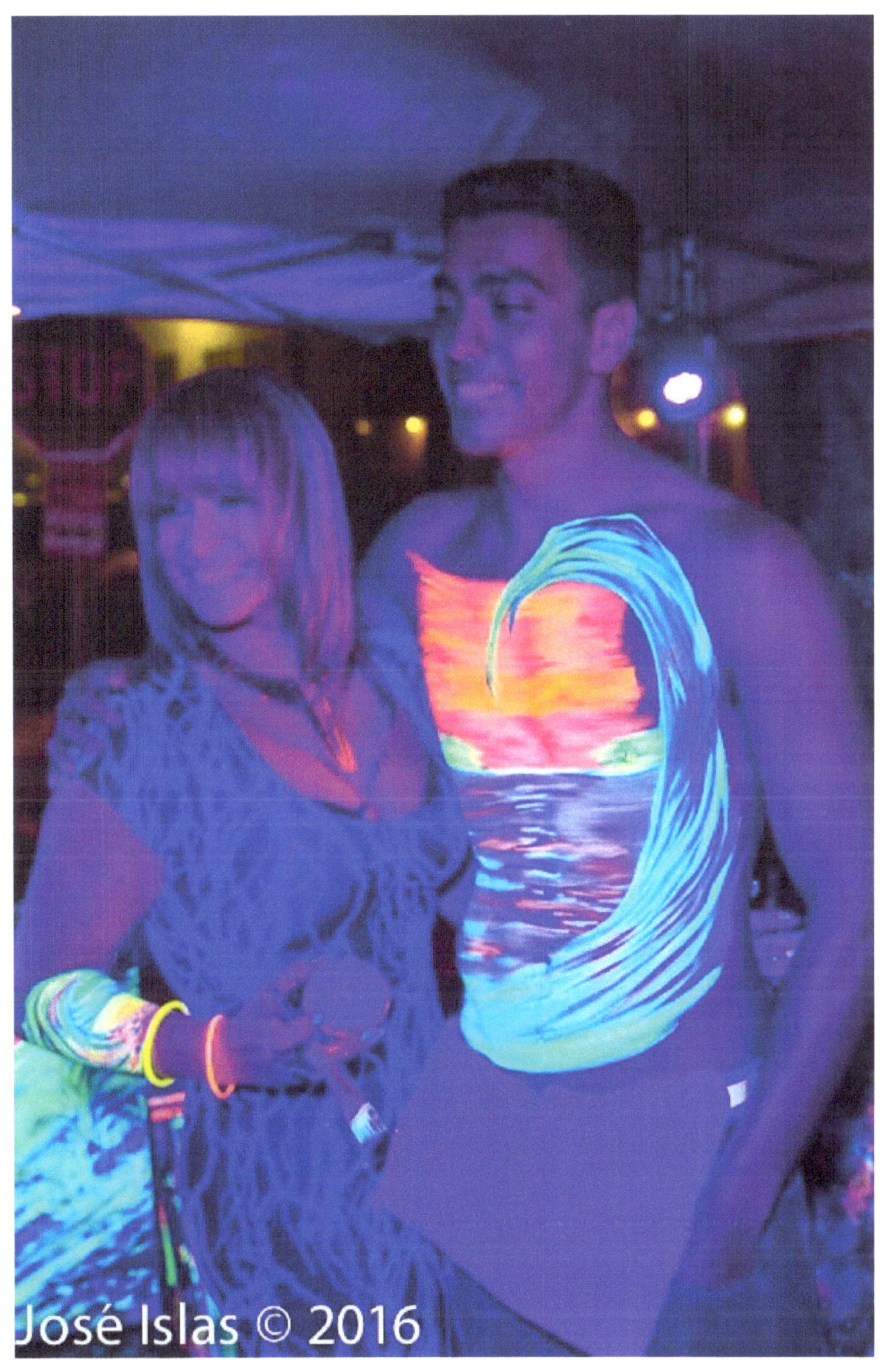

José Islas © 2016

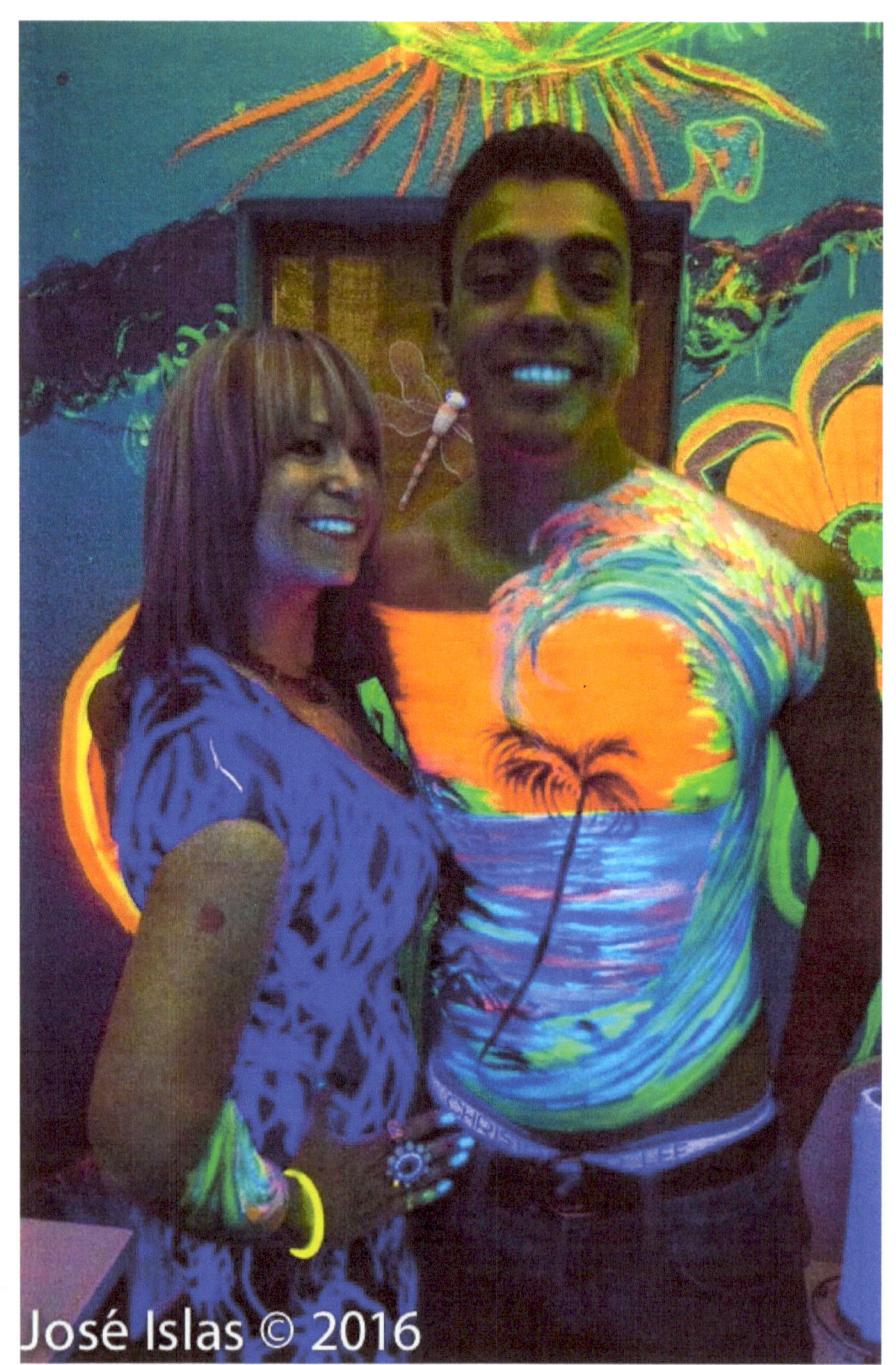

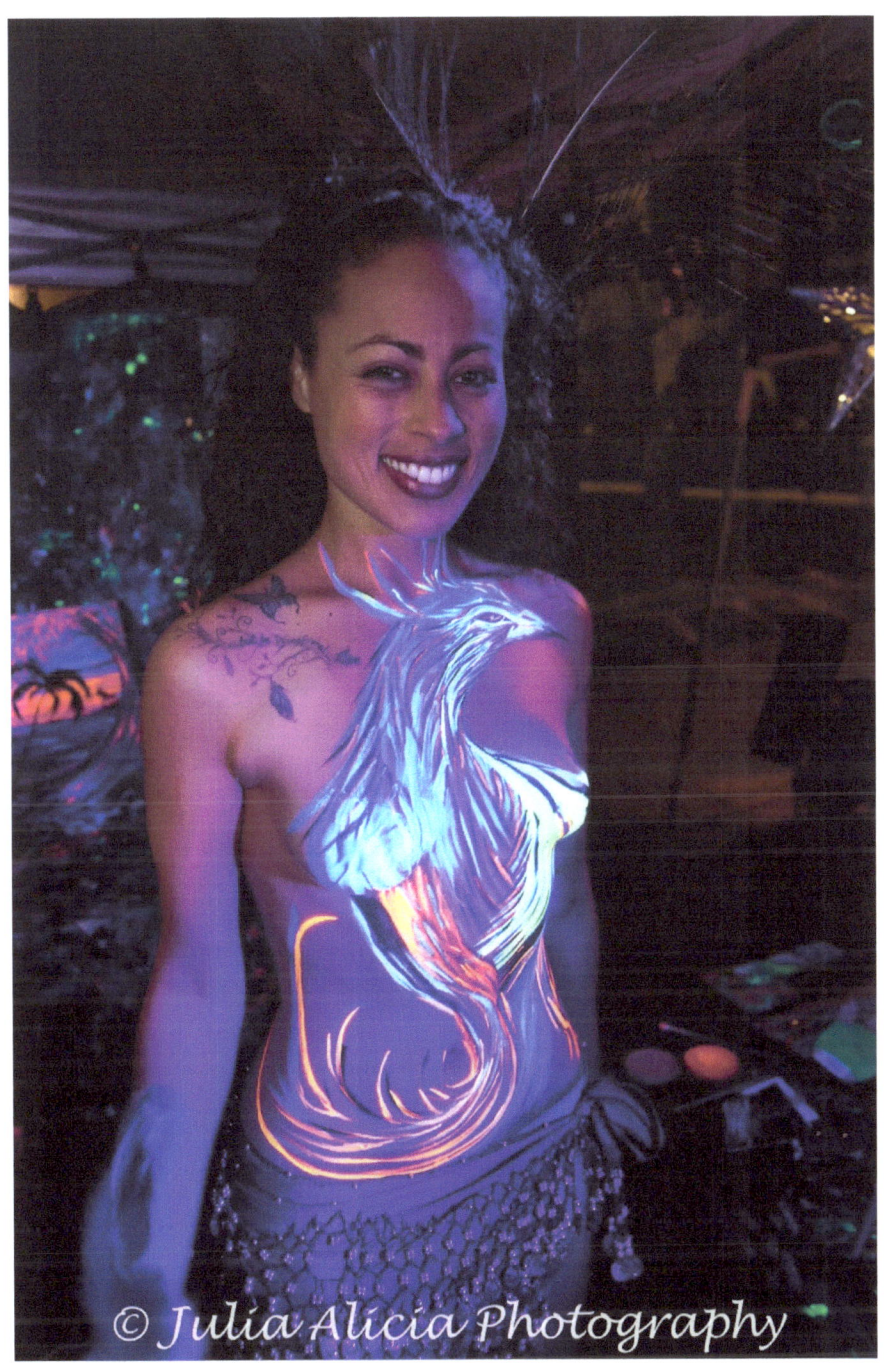

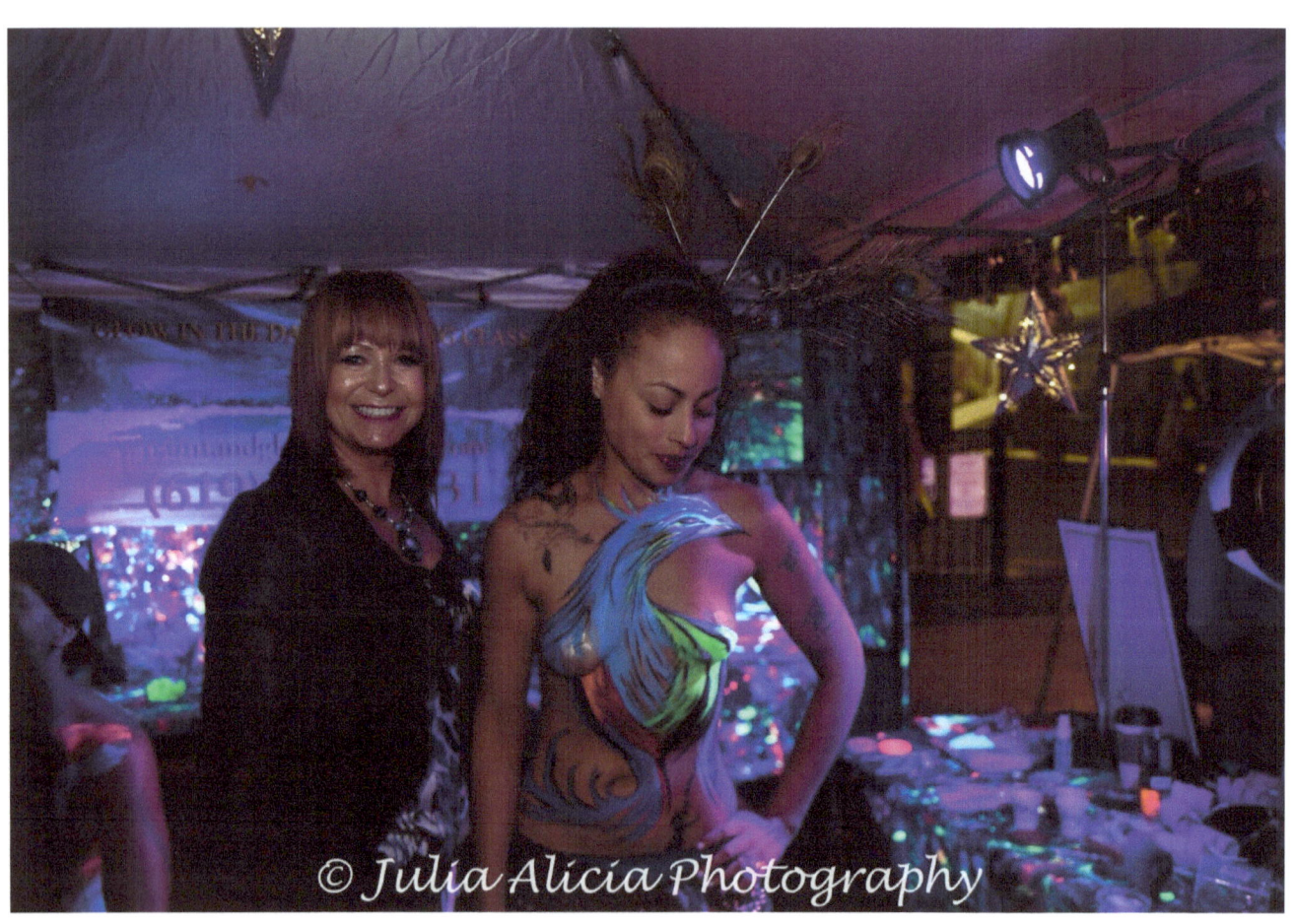

© Julia Alicia Photography

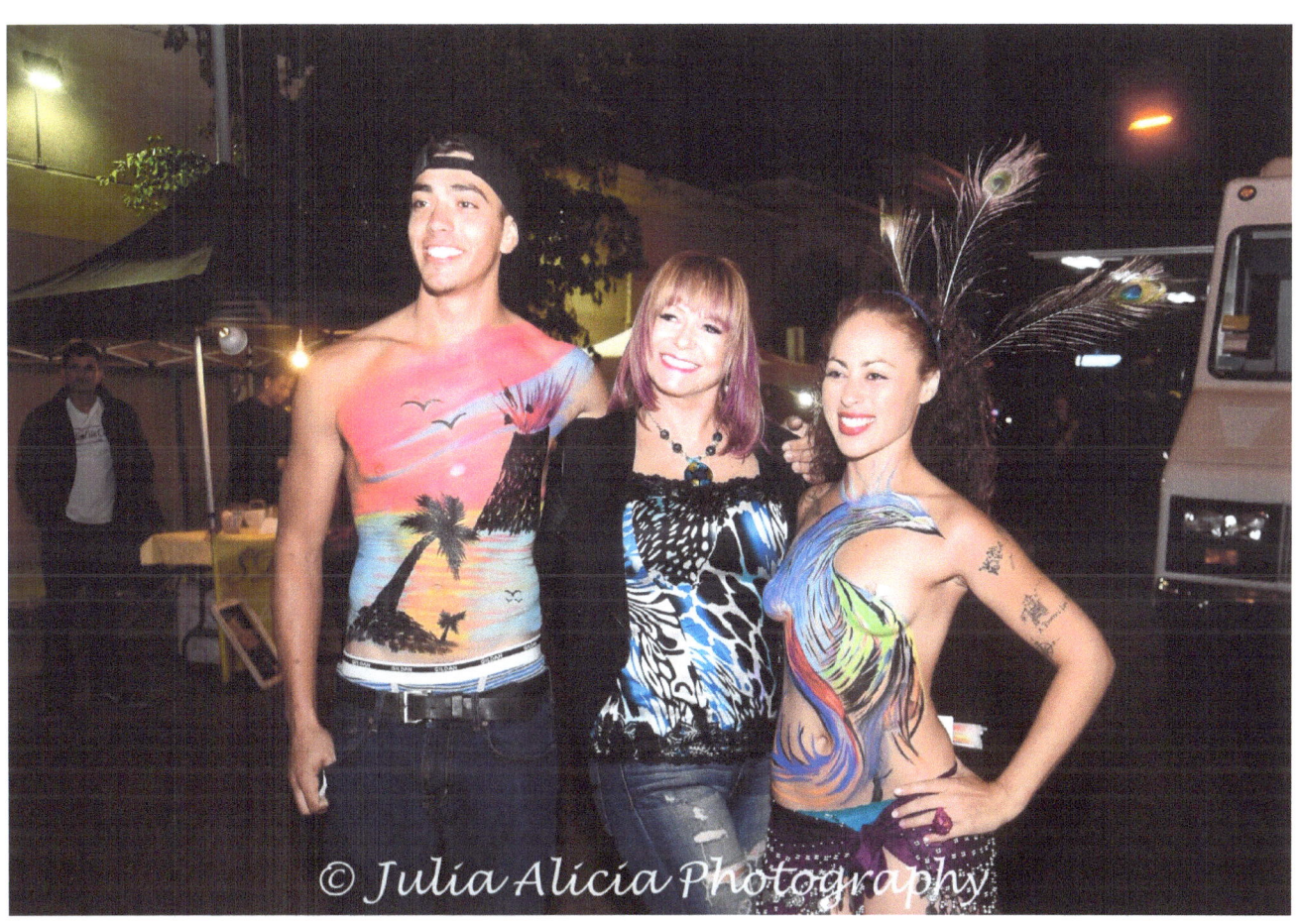

© Julia Alicia Photography

43

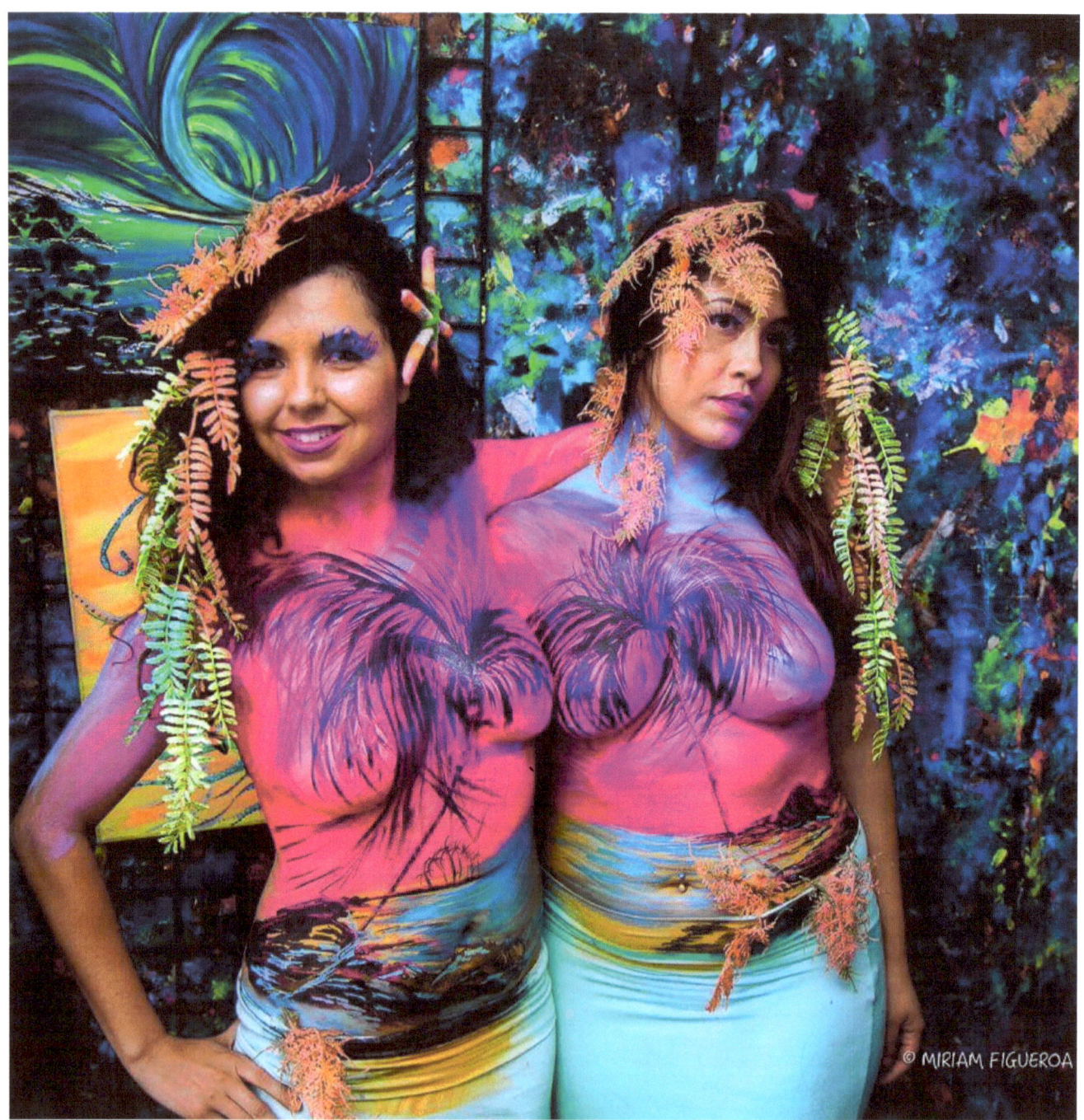

© MIRIAM FIGUEROA

44

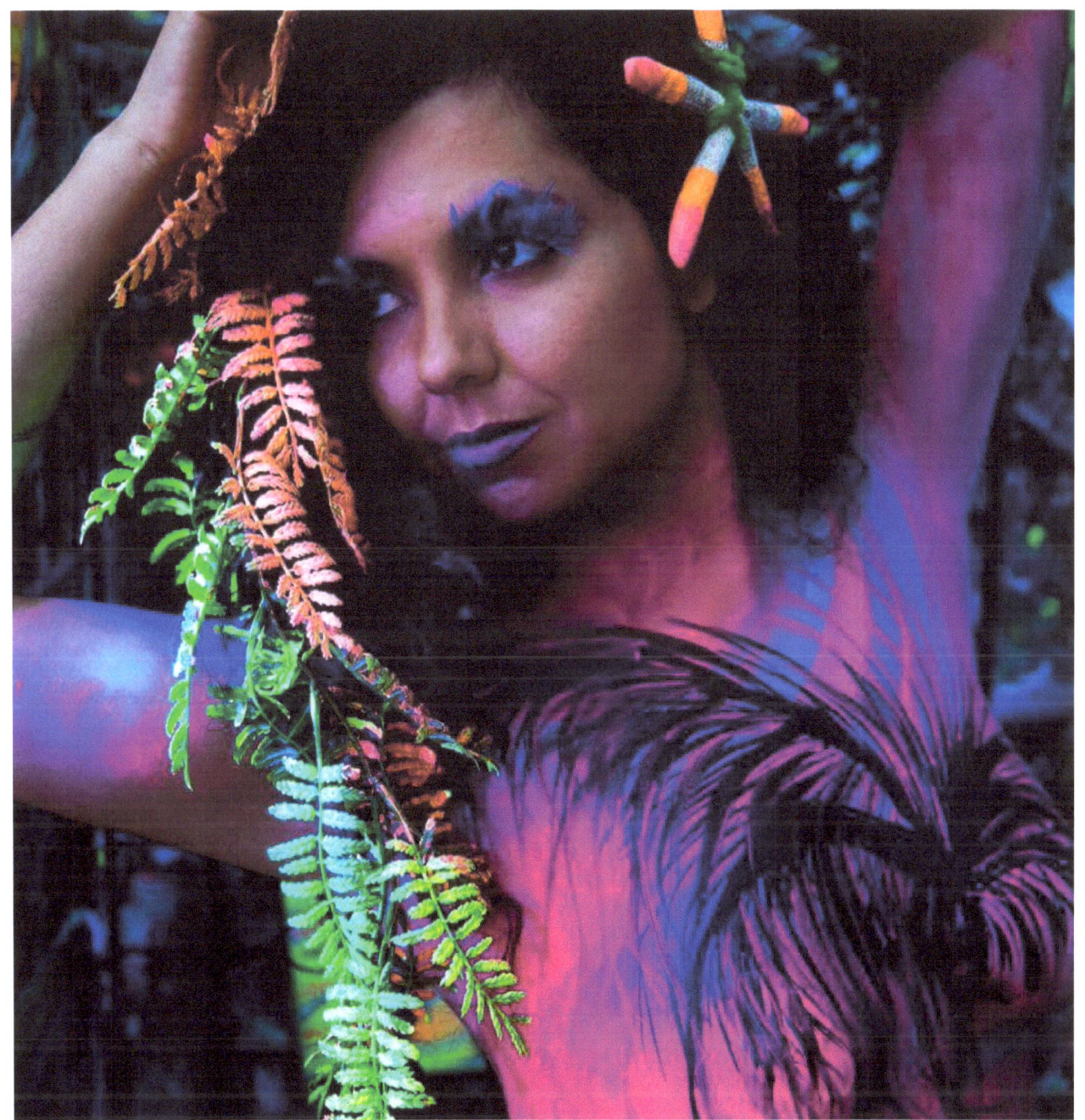

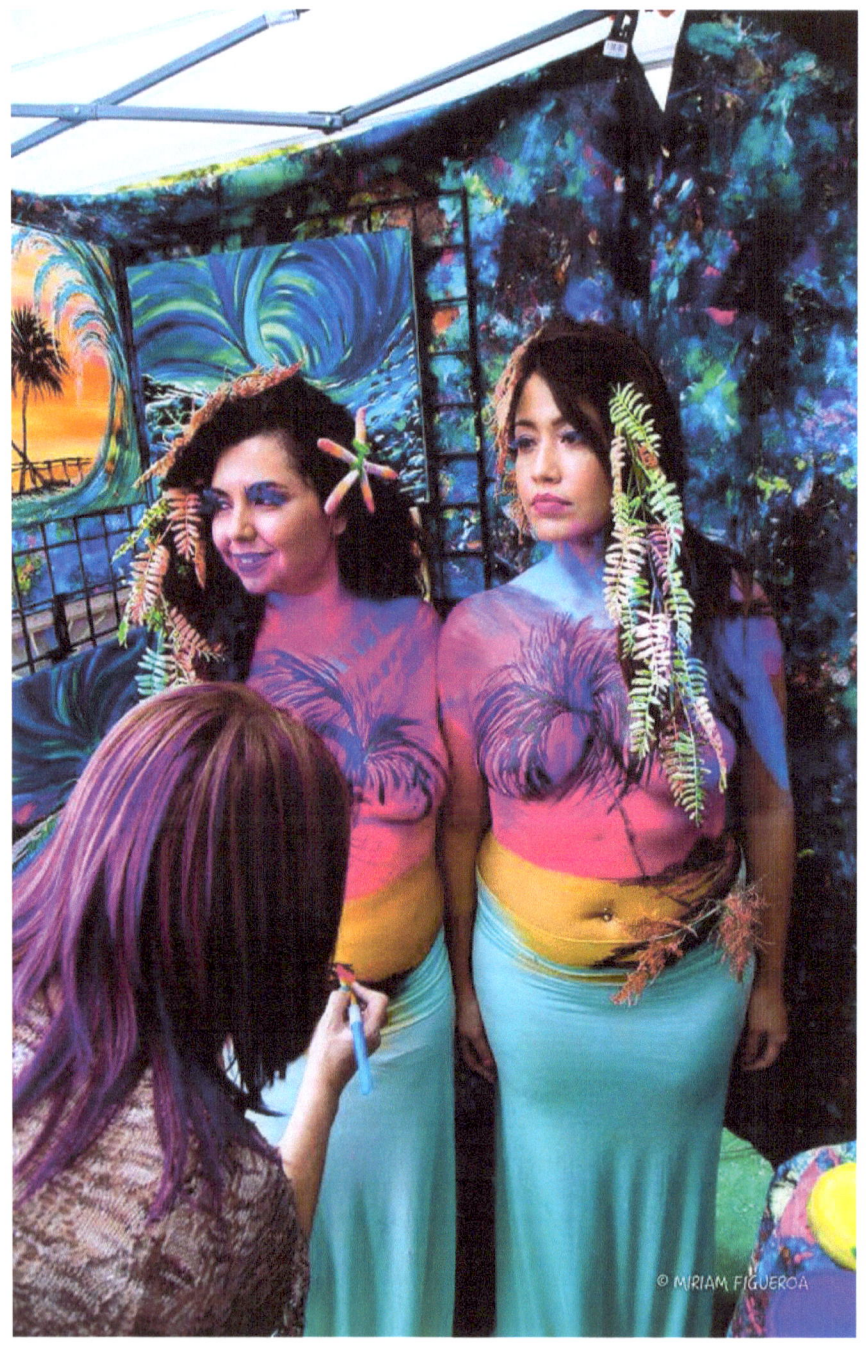

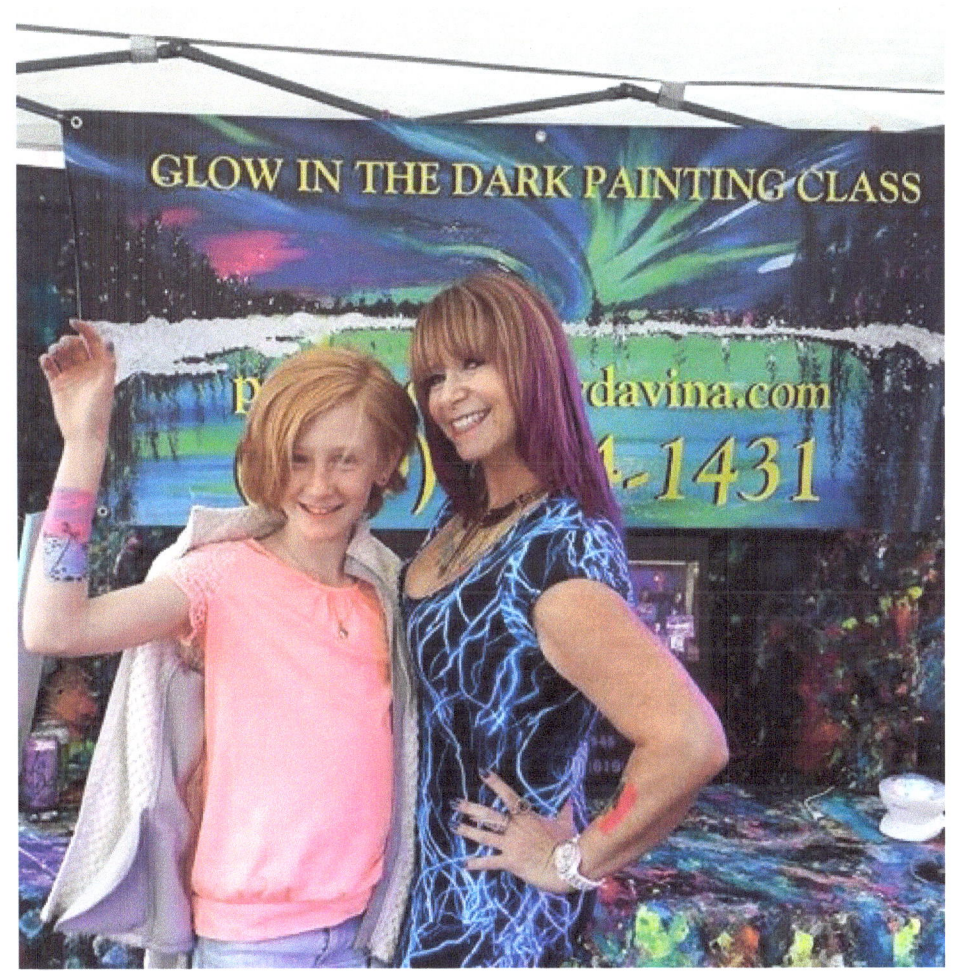

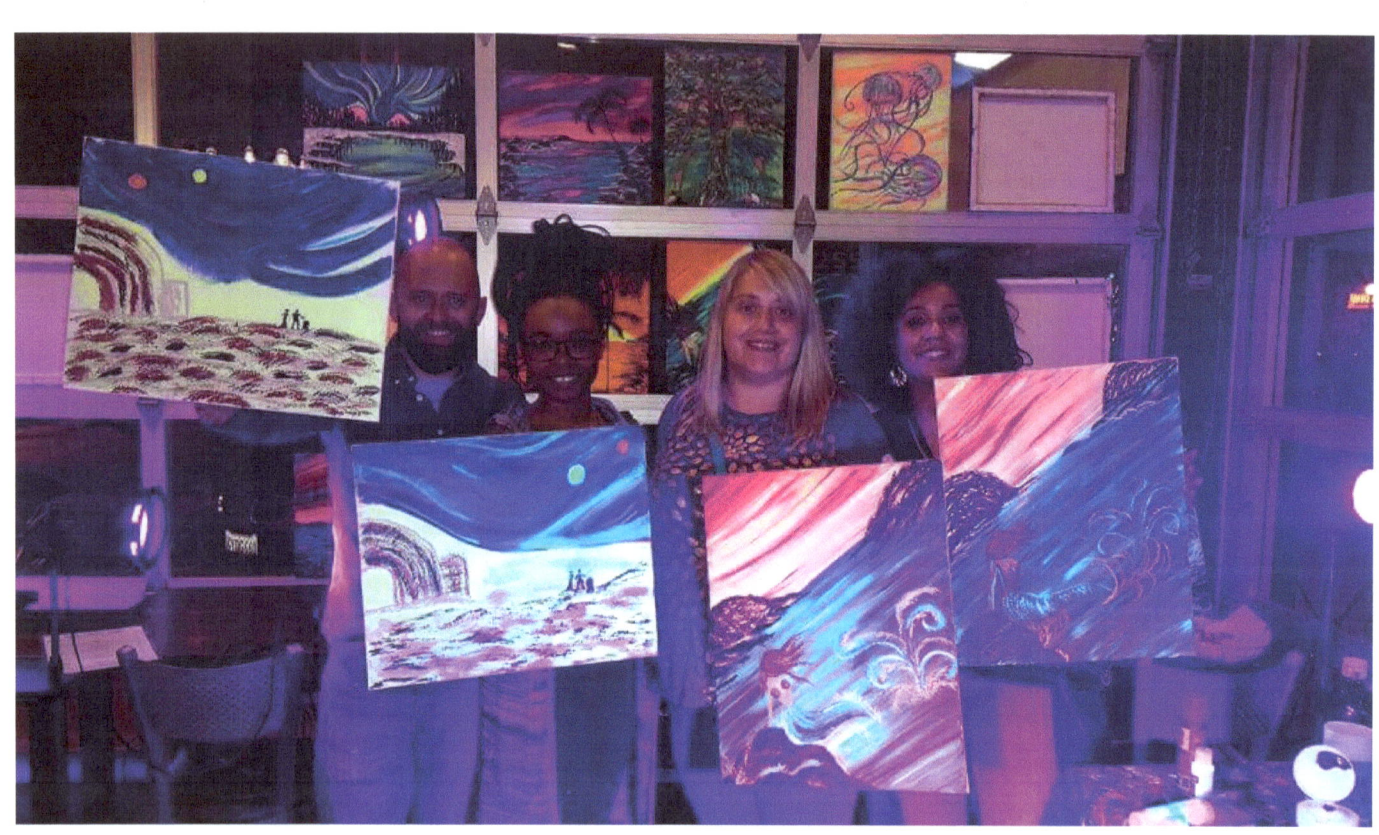

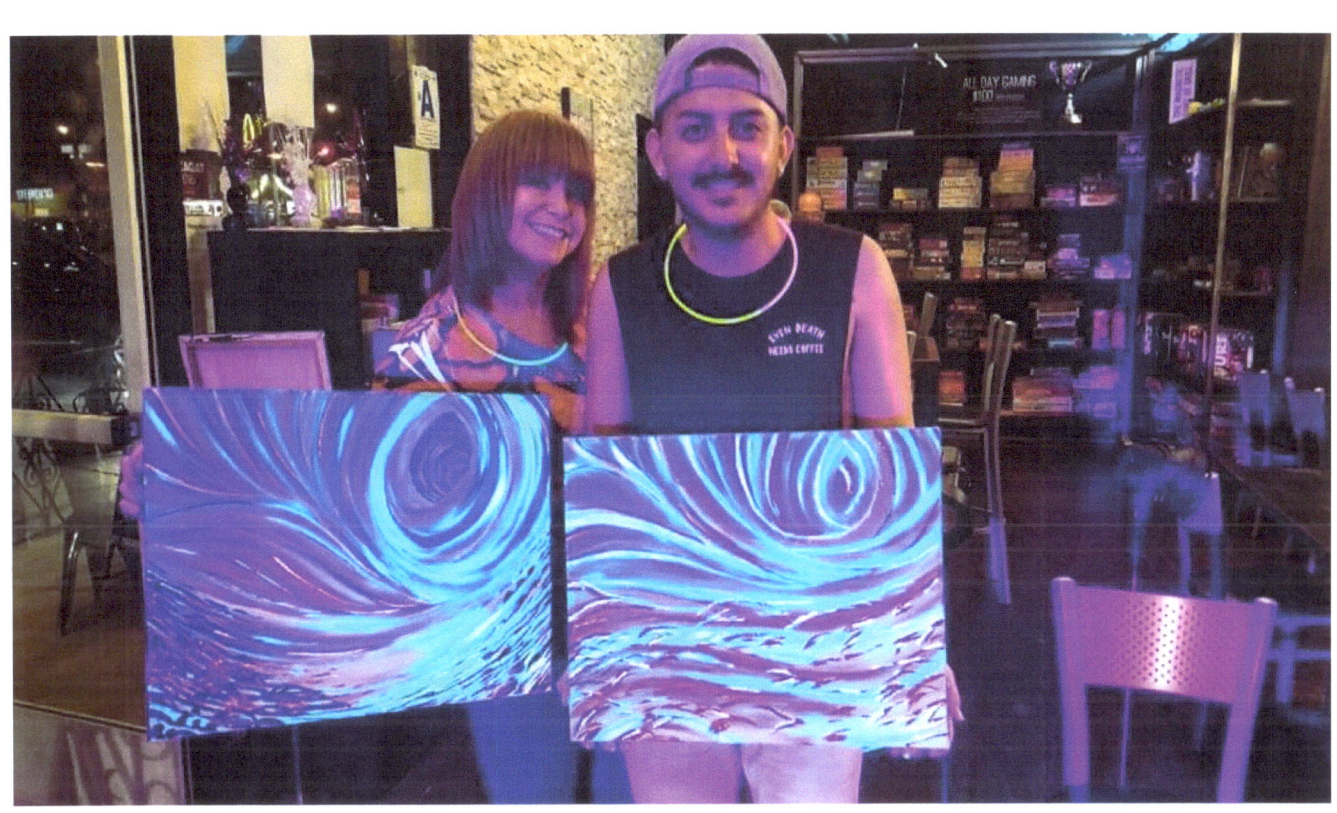

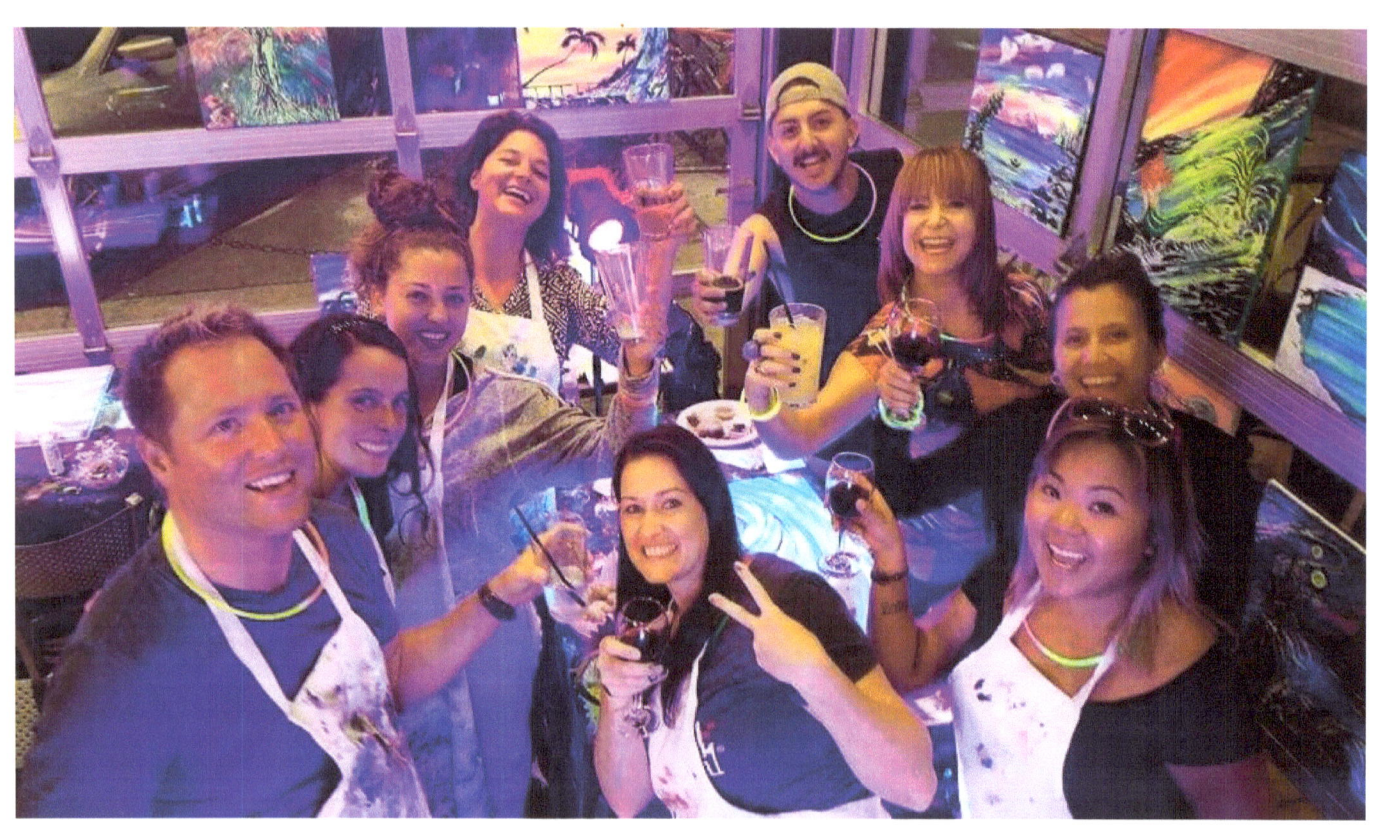

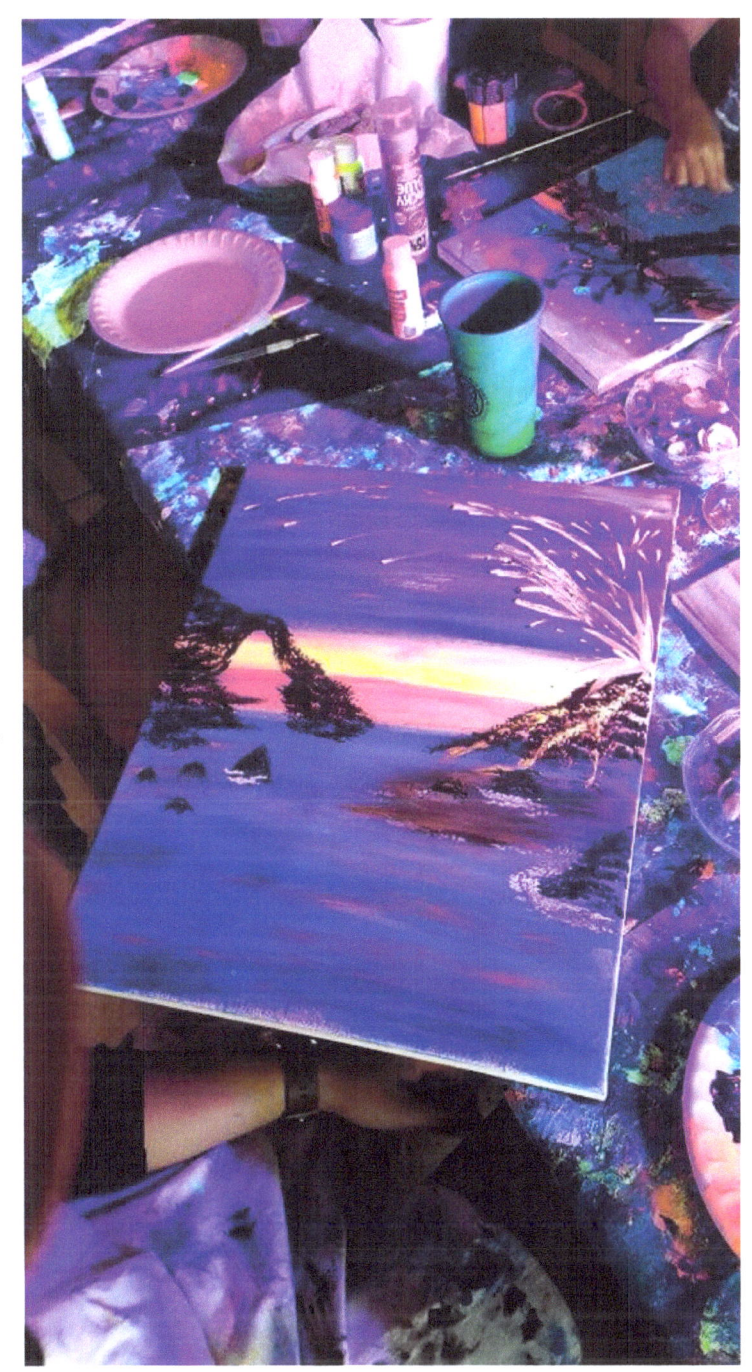

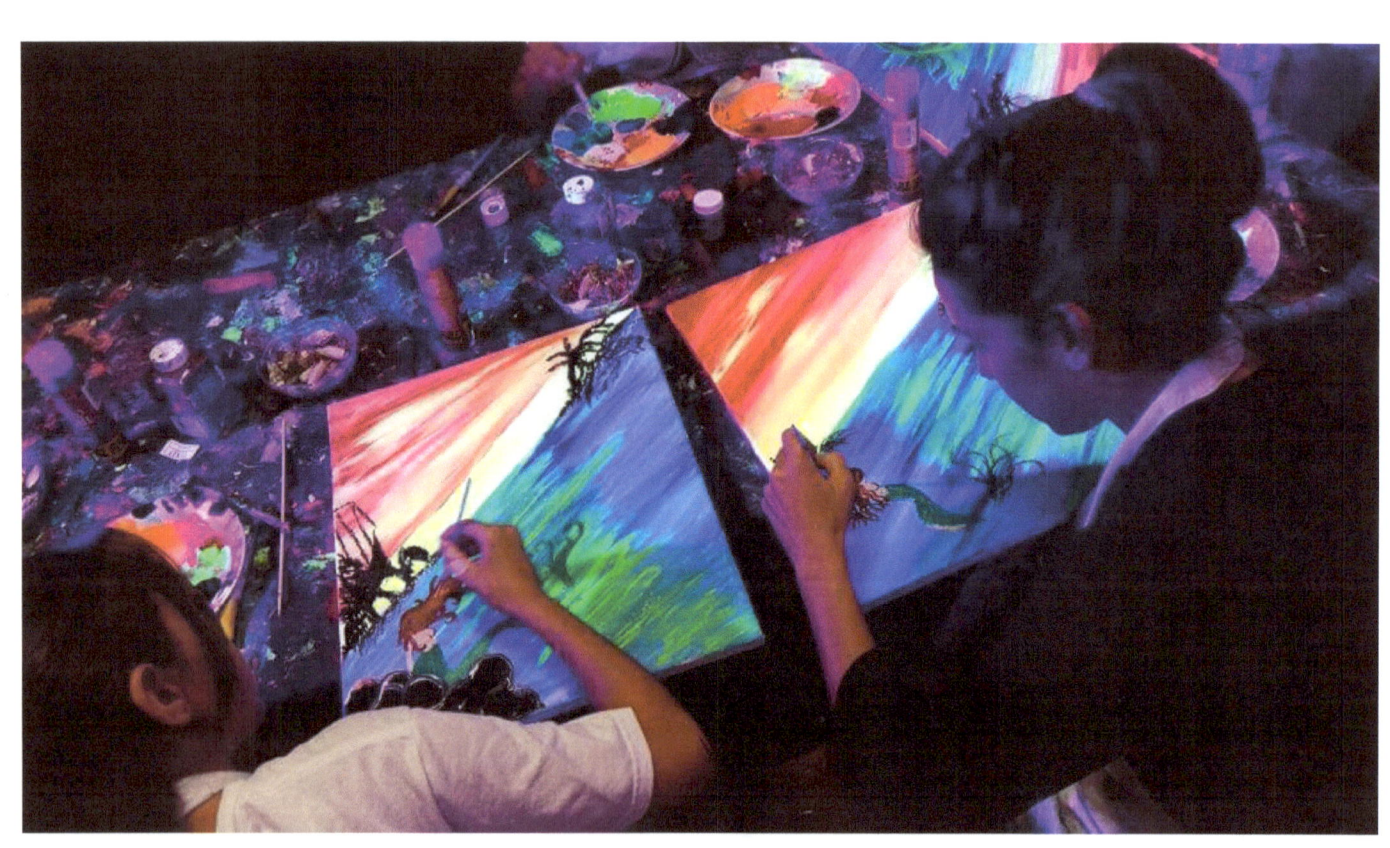

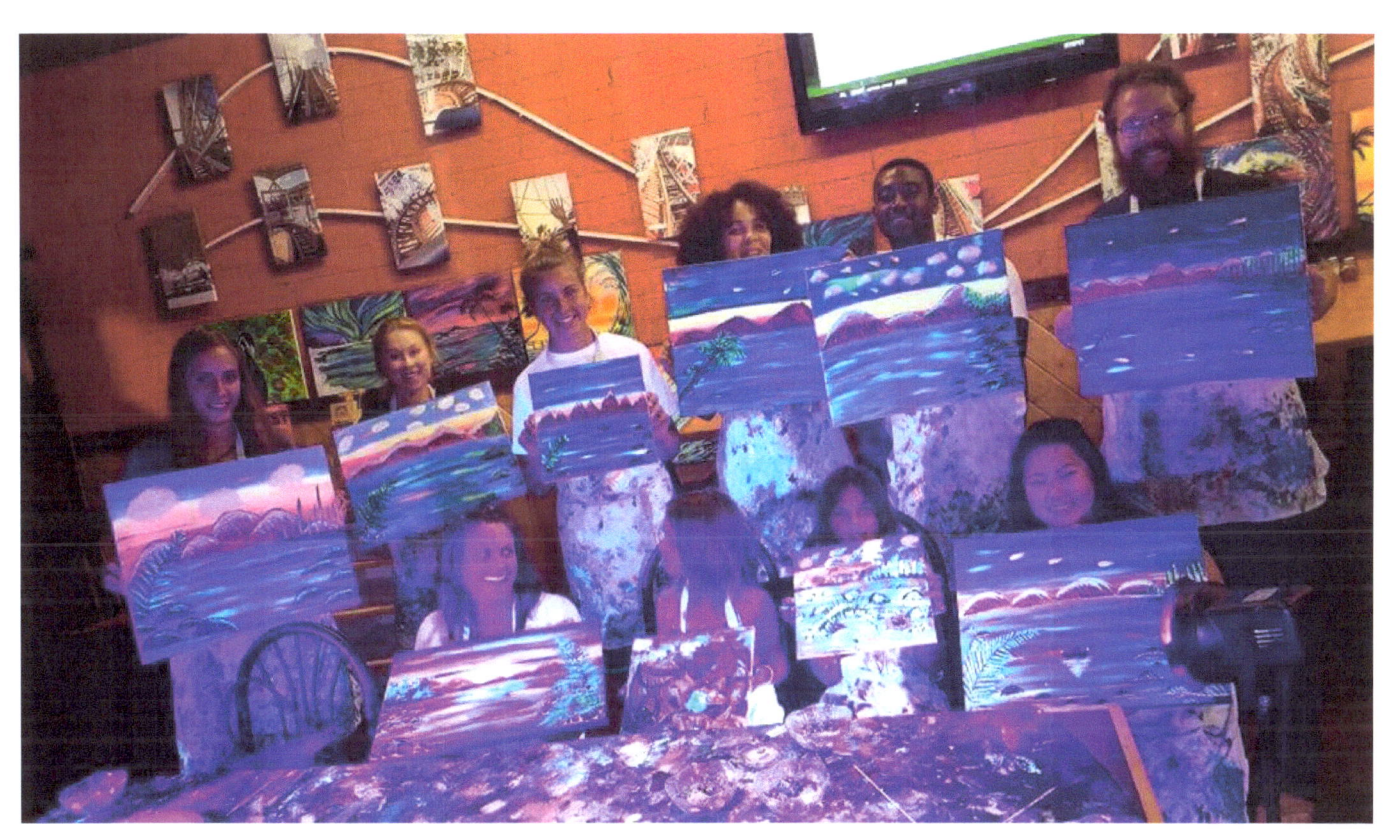

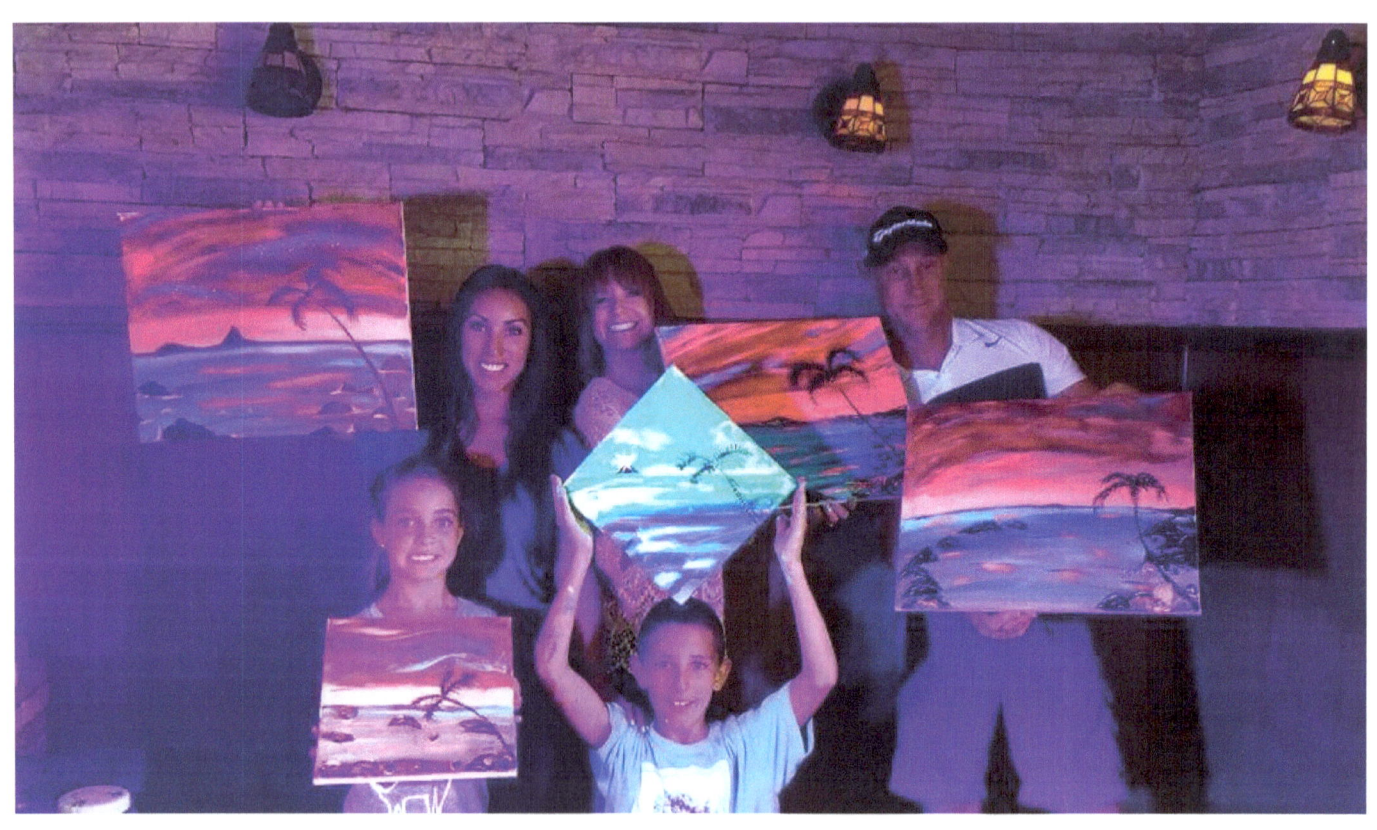

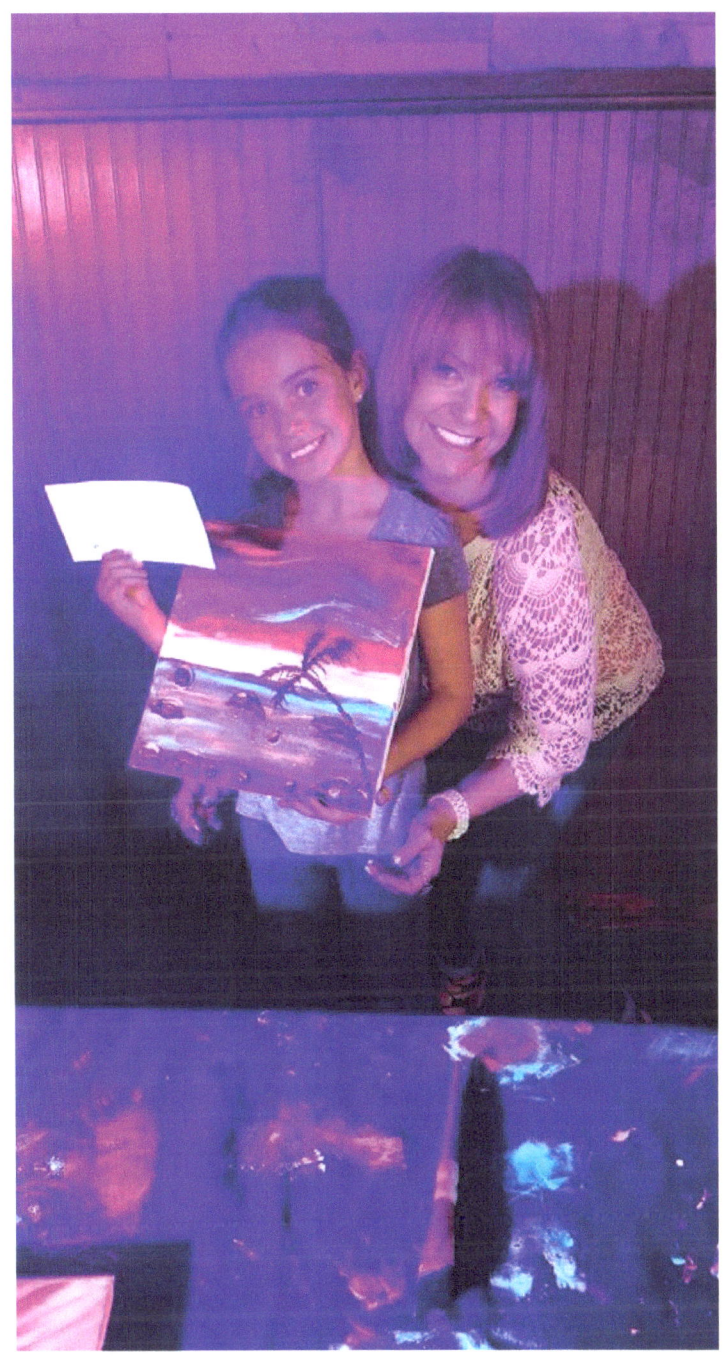

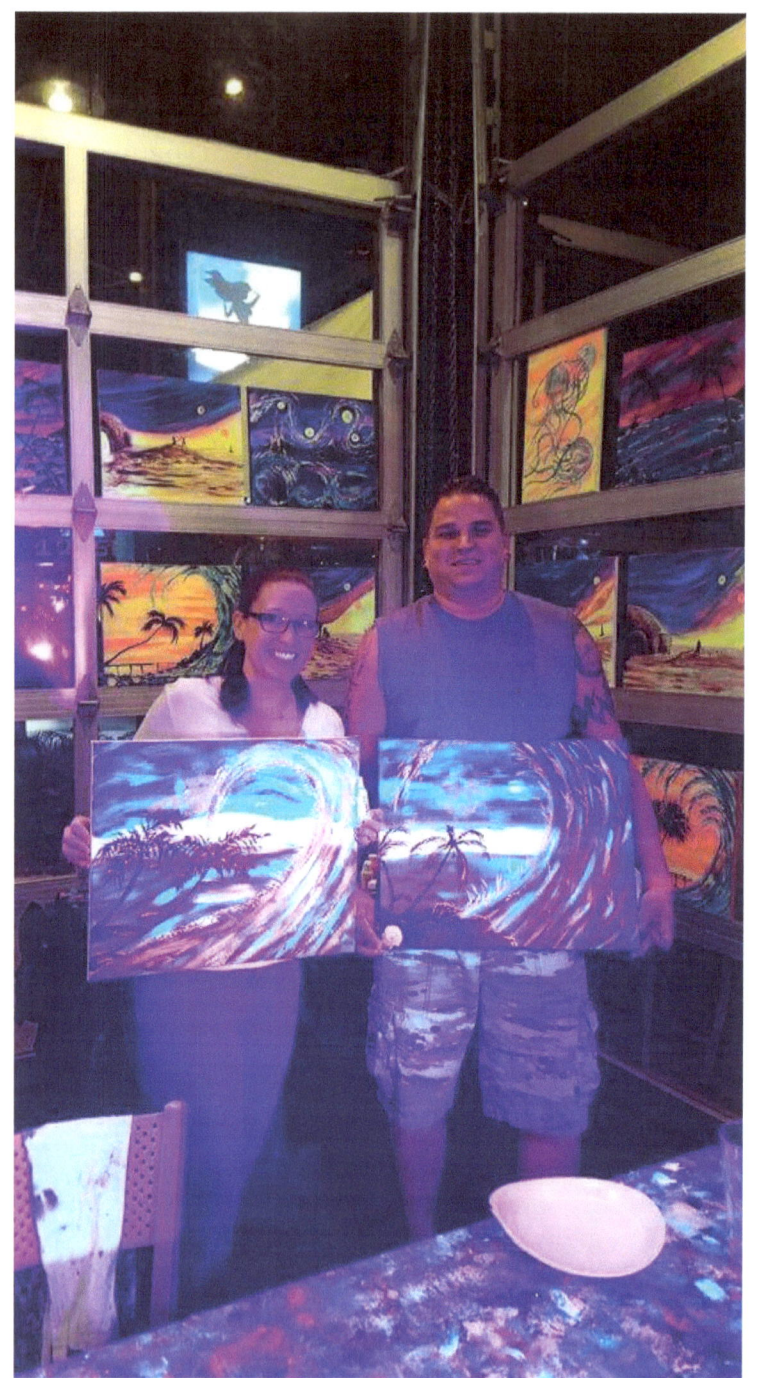

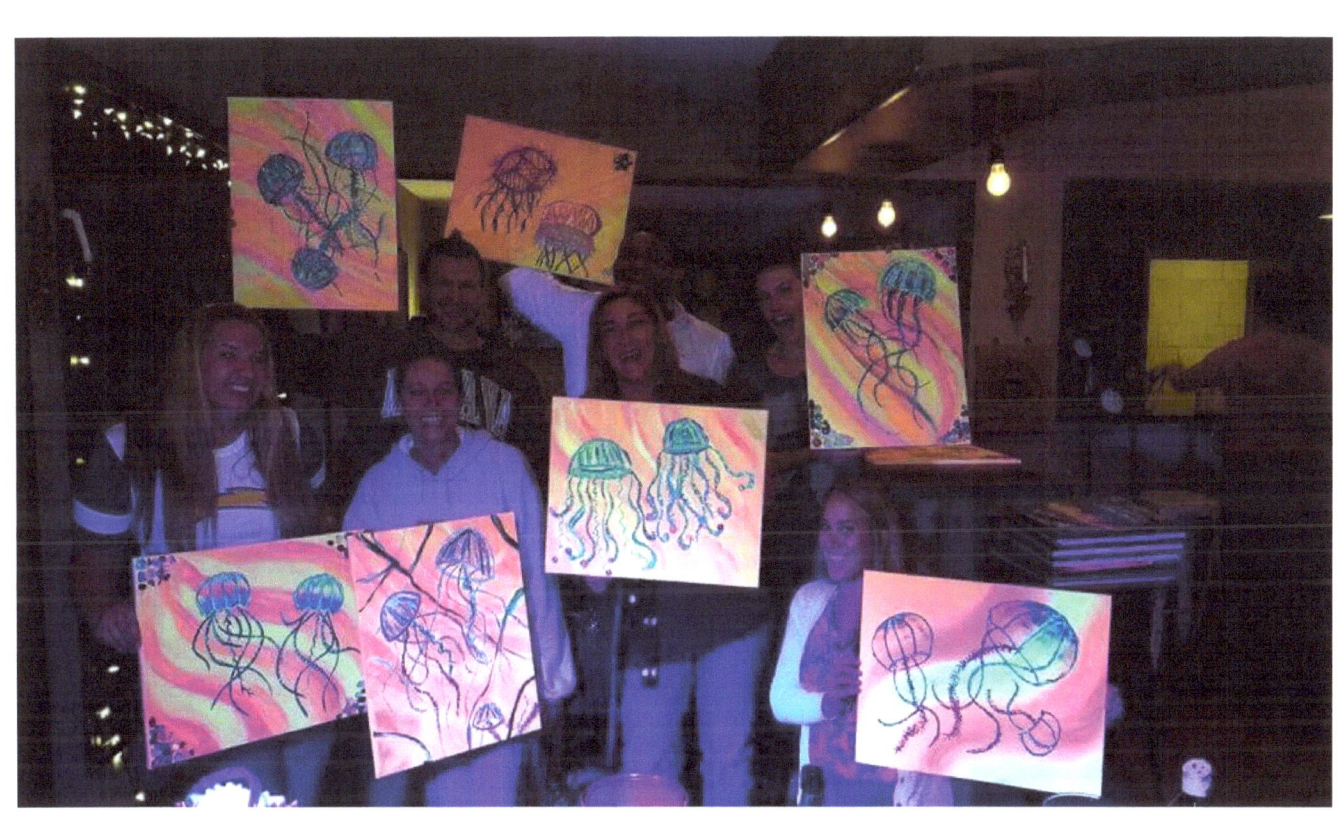

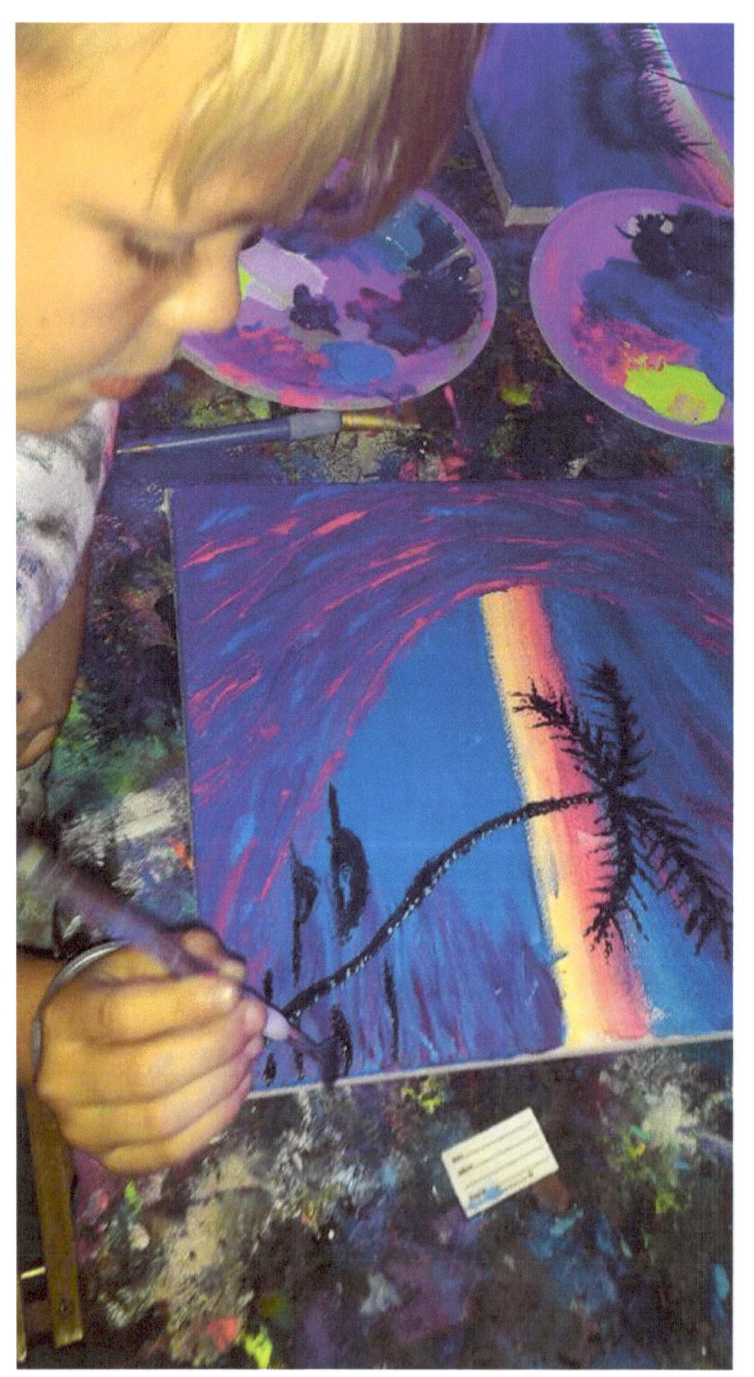

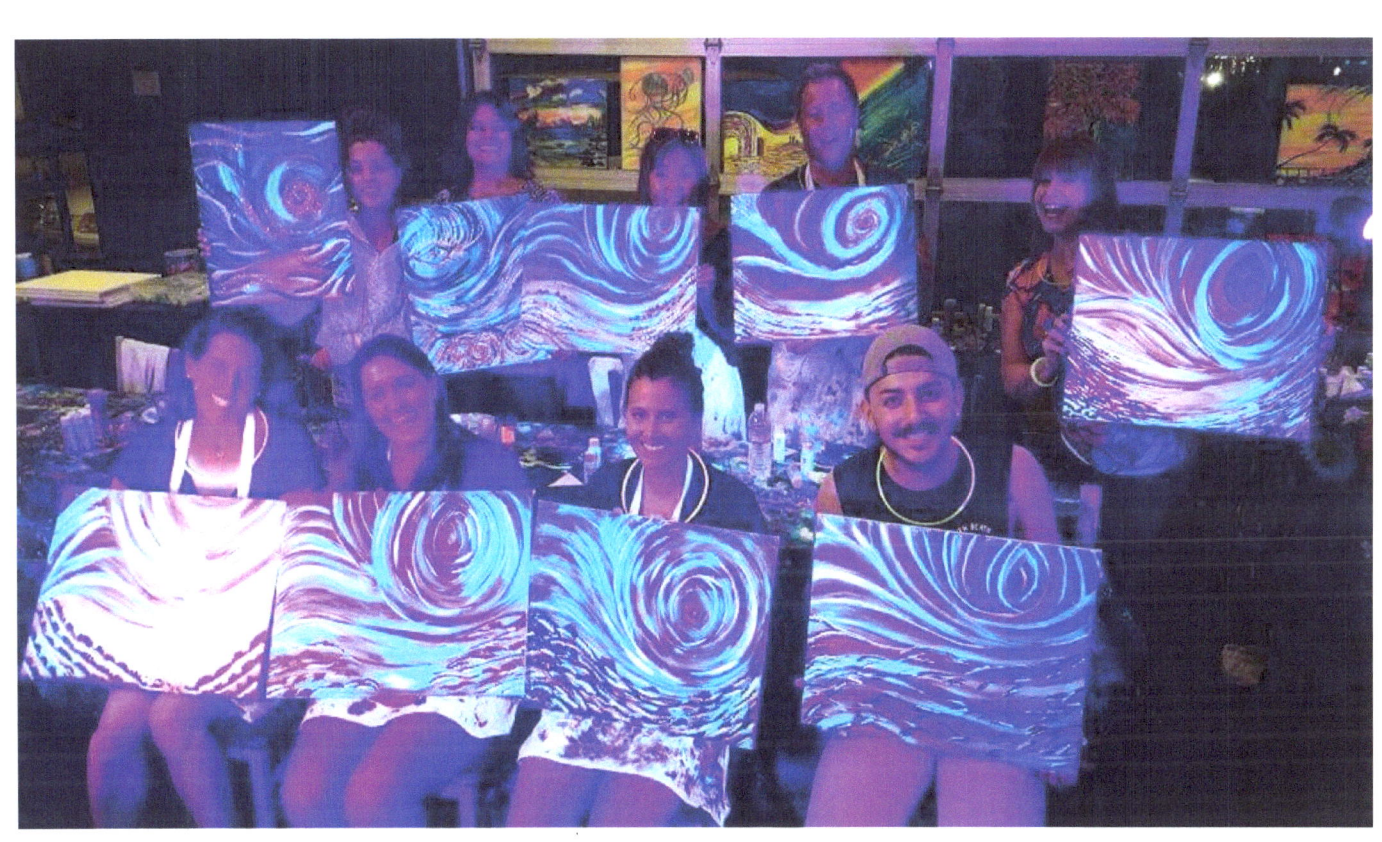

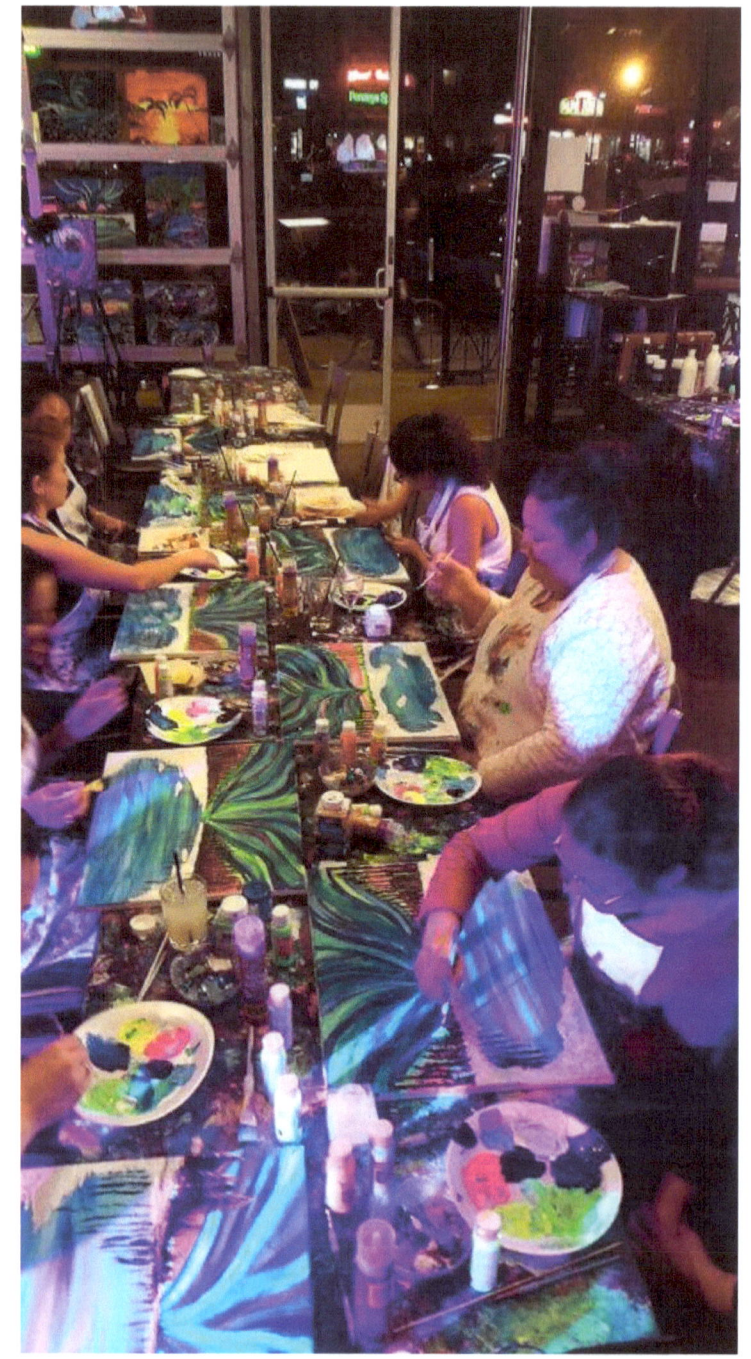

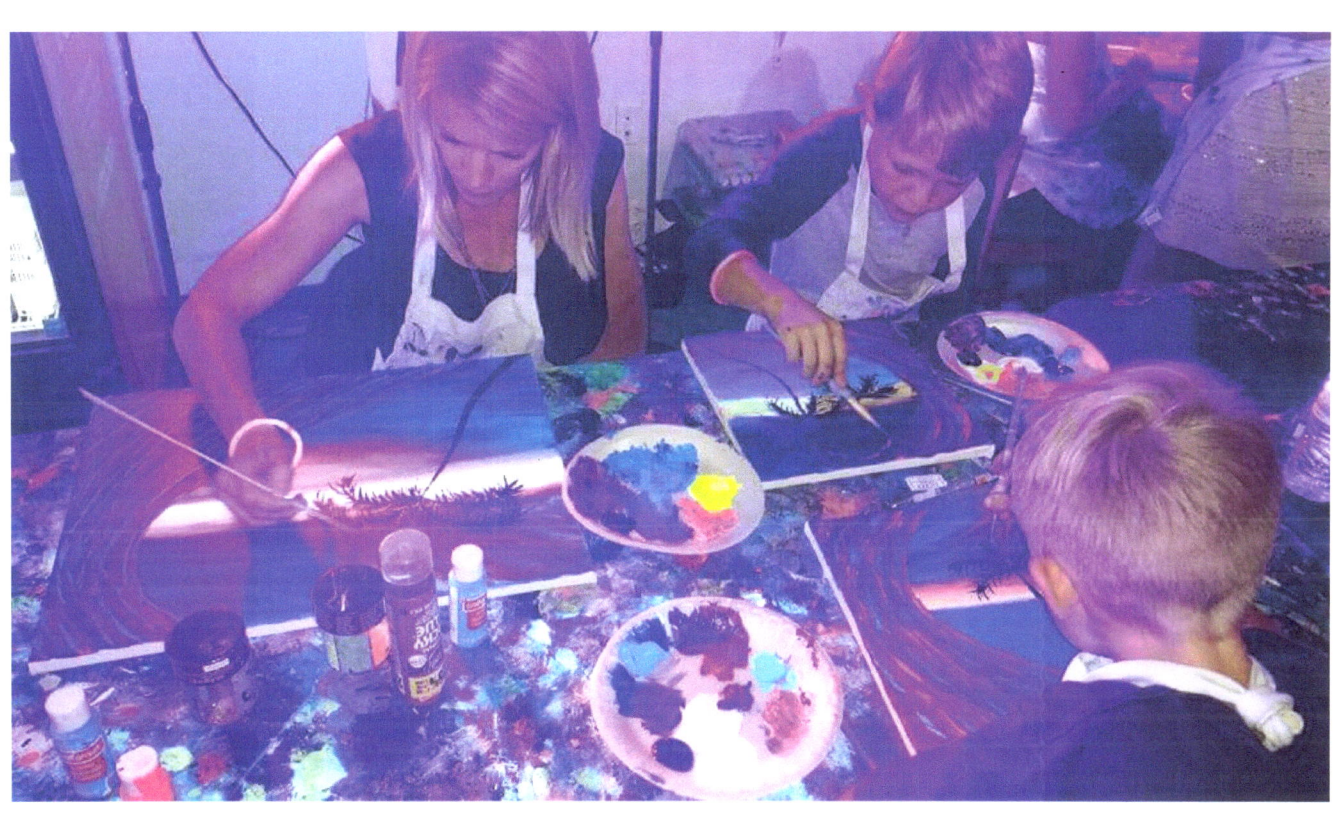

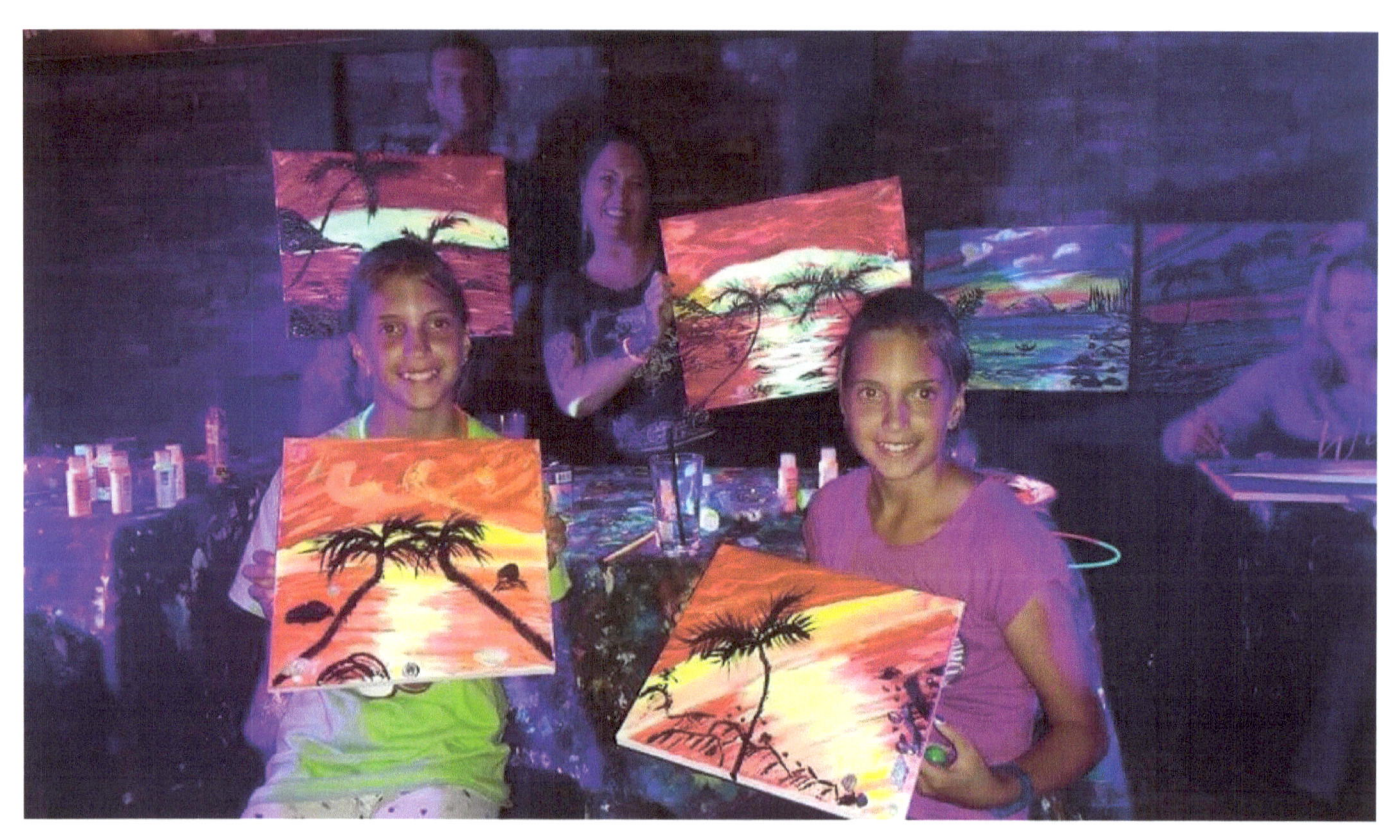

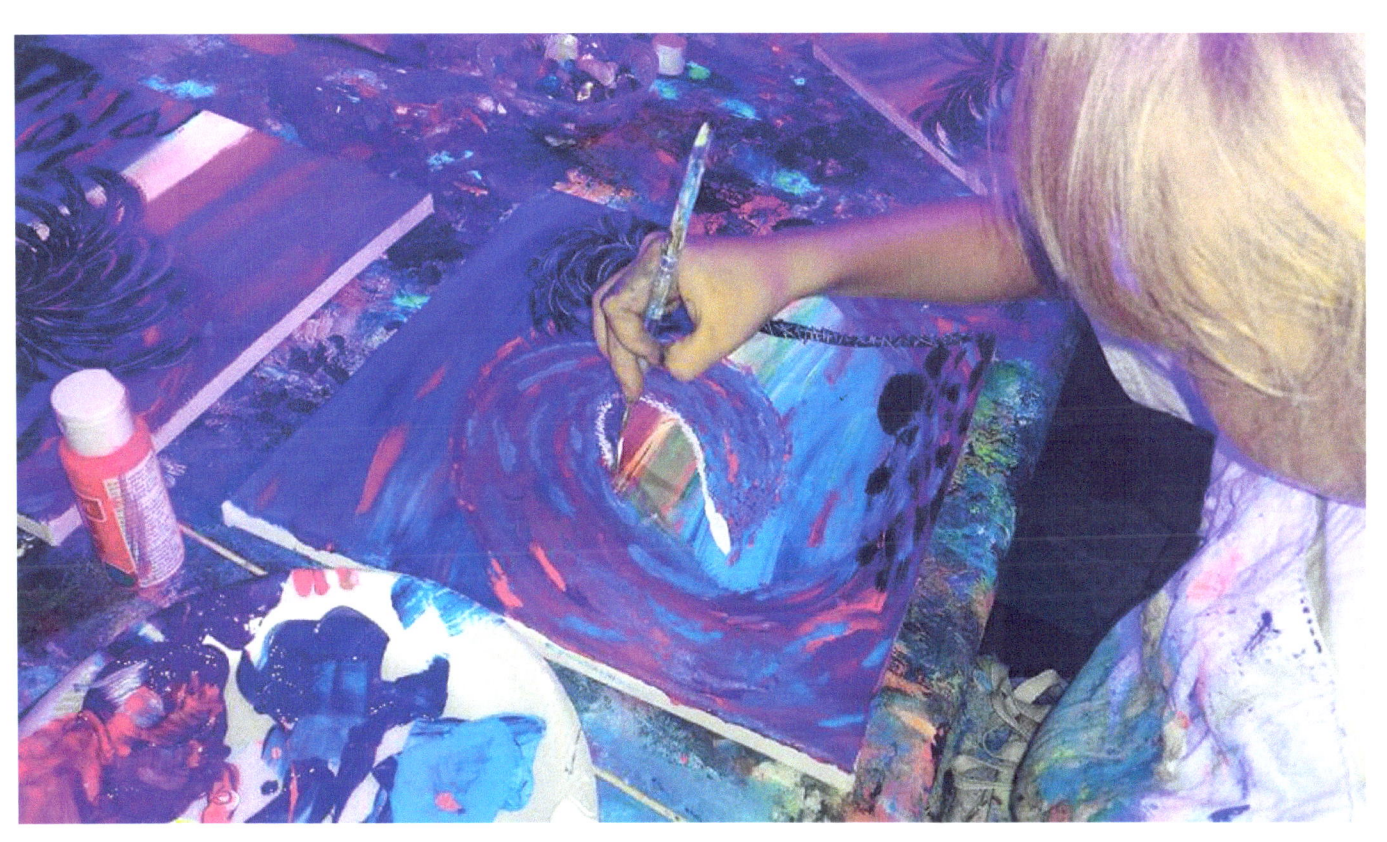

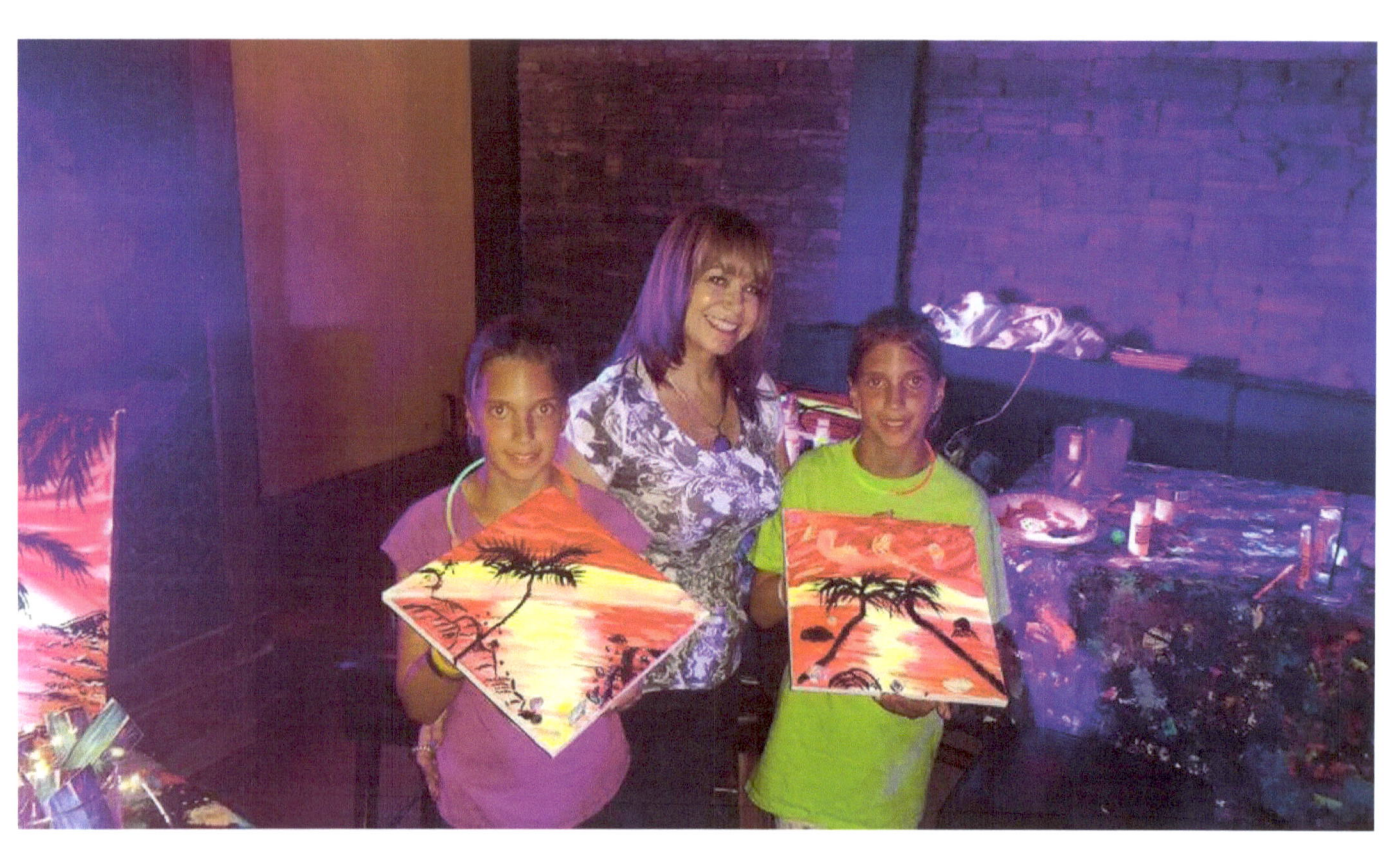

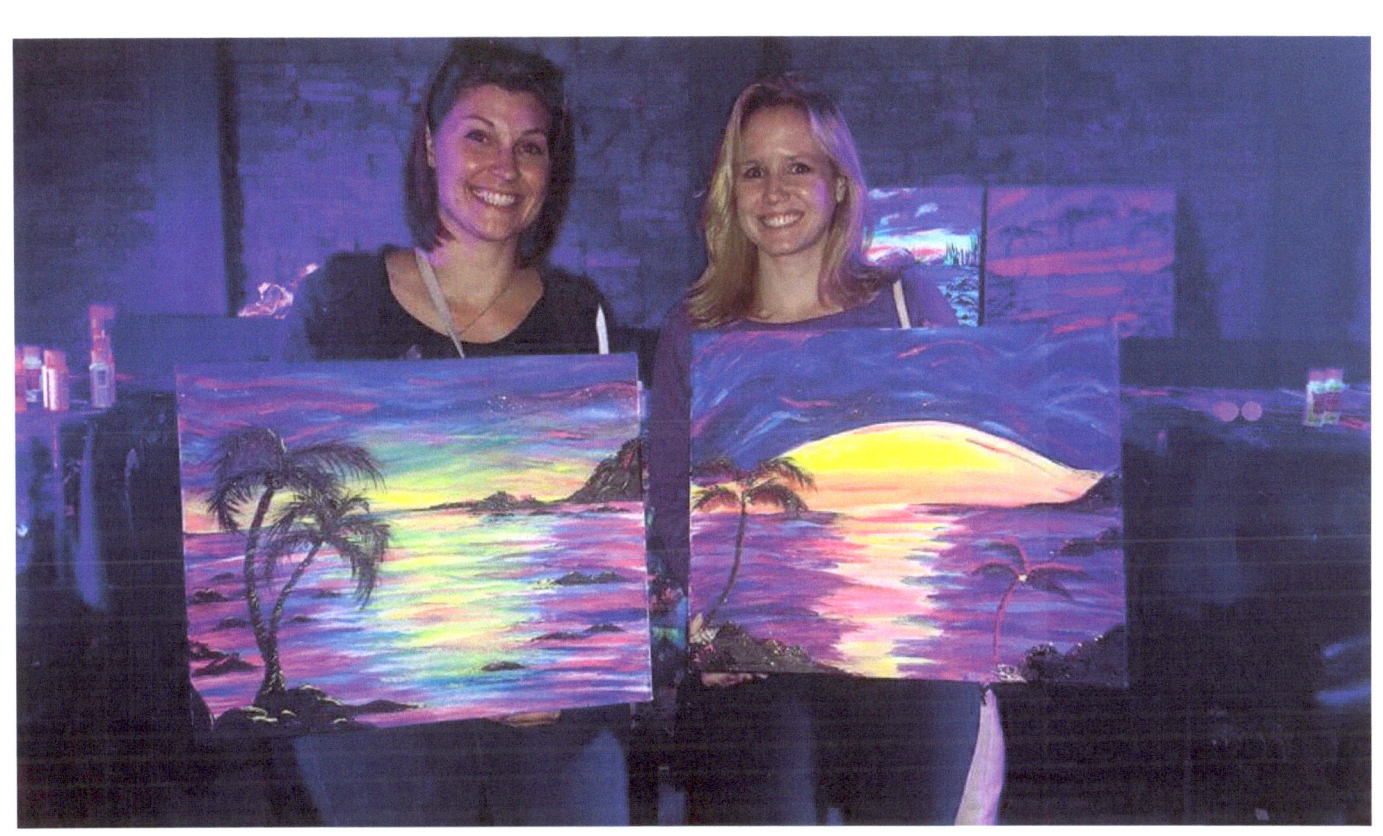

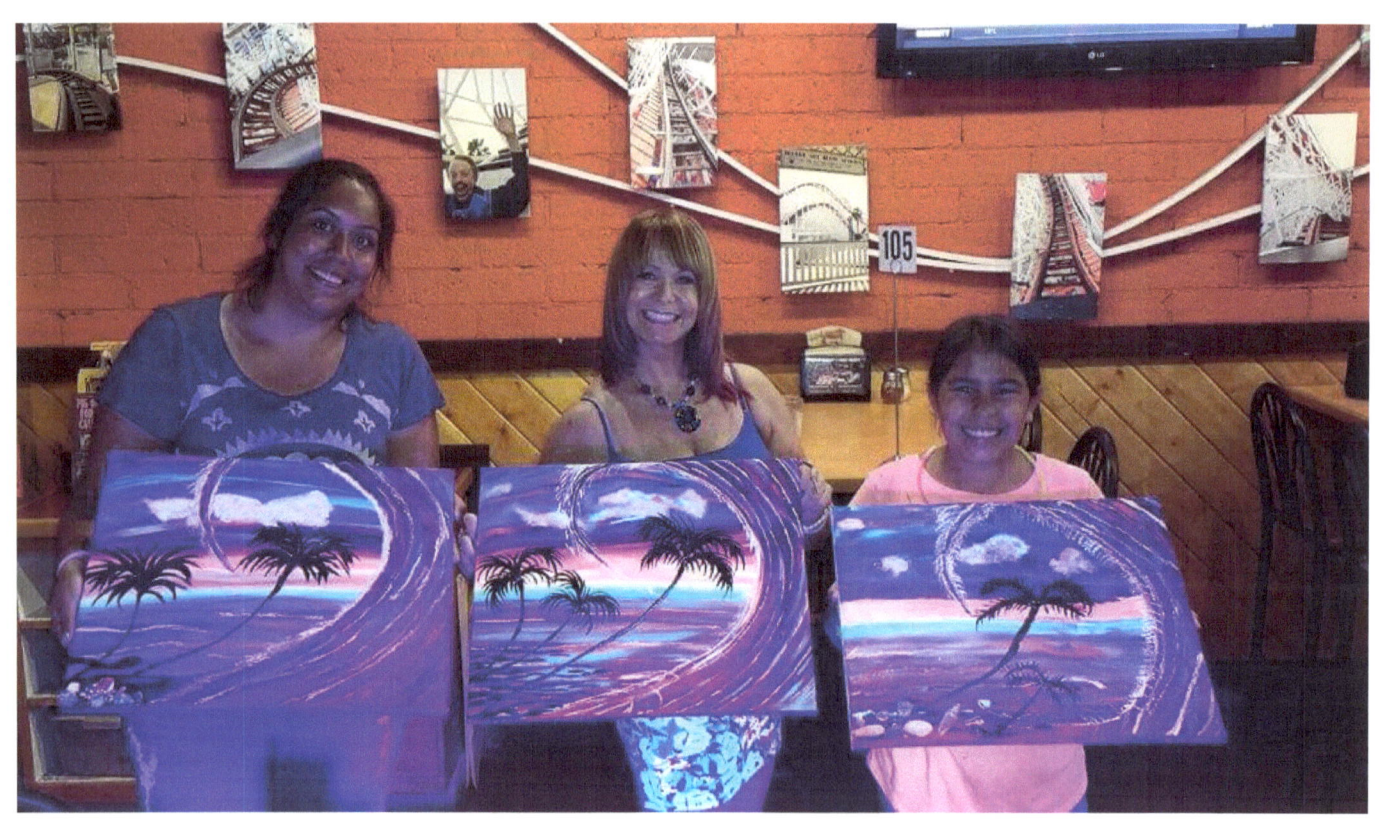

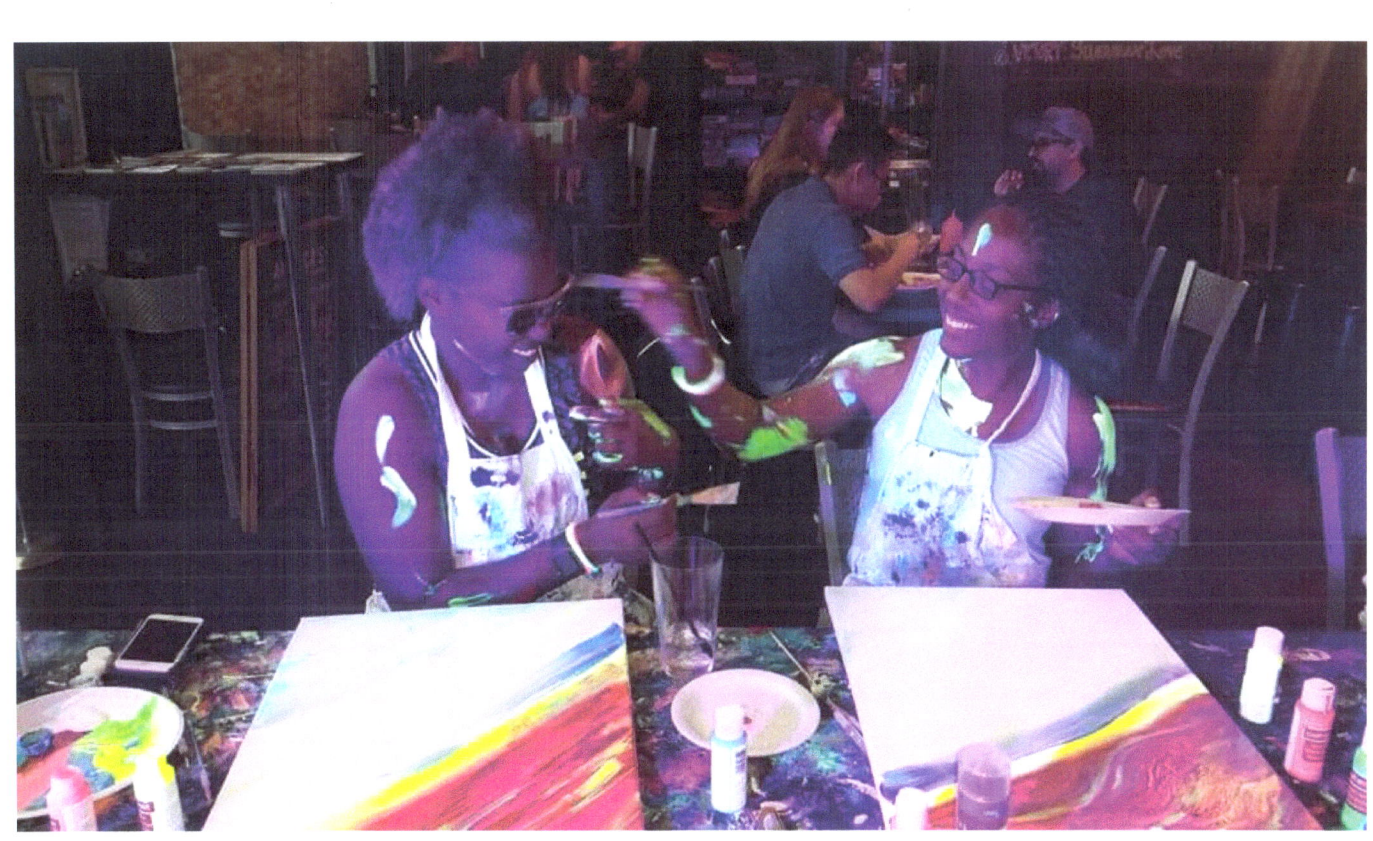

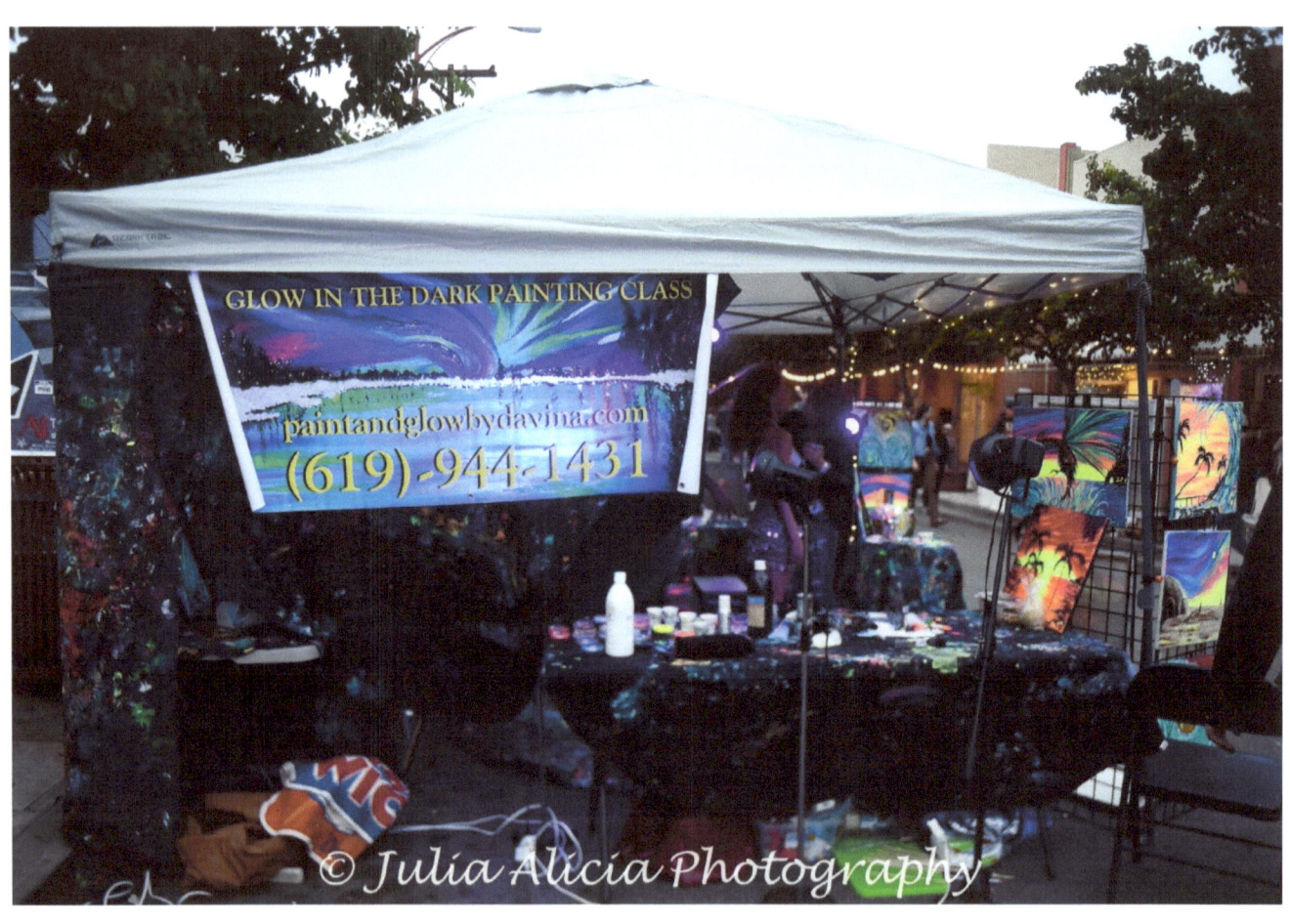

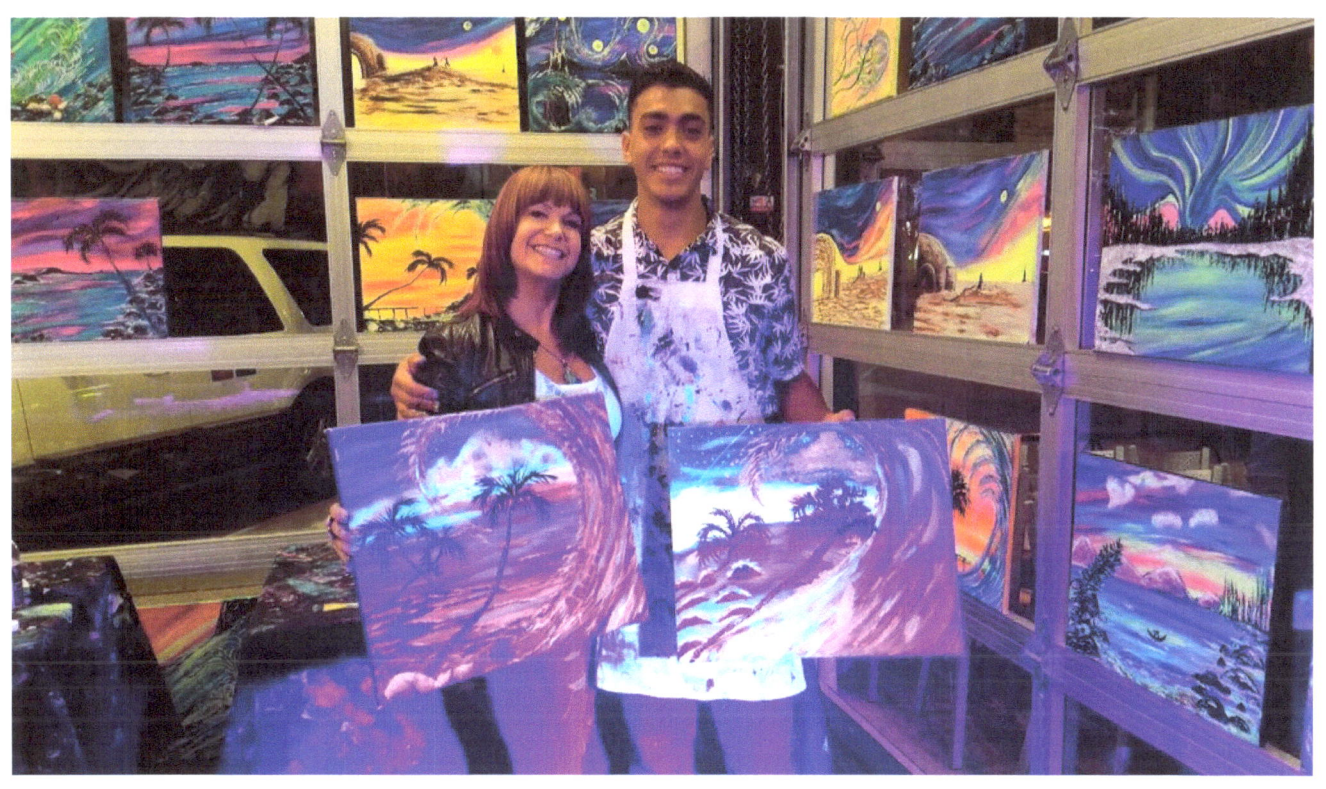

ABOUT THE AUTHOR

Born in Petaluma, California during the early 1970's, Bradley Zink grew up with a passion for books. Instilled in him by his parents, and surrounded with a library of books by Dr. Seuss, Mark Twain and Charles Dickens, to name a few, he developed a true passion for reading.

After the birth of his son, Alex, and being a stay-at-home dad, he too instilled the power of reading in his son. Using Dr. Seuss as the building blocks for teaching him, Bradley aspired to create a book for Alex, and all children to enjoy. With his son as his muse and inspiration, Bradley is constantly testing out his writings on the world's harshest critic, his son Alex.

www.ingramcontent.com/pod-product-compliance
Lightning Source LLC
Chambersburg PA
CBHW050741180526
45159CB00003B/1305